Prodigal Pilgrim

Letters to Pope Francis from Lourdes, Fatima, Garabandal and Medjugorje

Peter Breen

En Route Books and Media, LLC

St. Louis, MO, USA

D1267468

ENROUTE
Make the time

NIHIL OBSTAT – Dr Chris Geraghty DD (Sydney), M Th (Paris)

Australian ISBN 978-0-646-852423
US ISBN 978-1-956715-13-2

LCCN: 2021951780

A catalogue record for this work is available from the National Library of Australia and in the Library of Congress in the United States.

Cover design: Judy Bullard www.customebookcovers.com

Image of Mary from the statue outside St James Church in Medjugorje © iStock

Send out your Spirit … and renew the face of the earth.

Psalm 104:30

Come, Holy Spirit, fill the hearts of your faithful,
And kindle in us the fire of your love.
Send forth your Spirit that we may be recreated,
And you shall renew the face of the earth.

Traditional Christian Prayer

Dear children … I am preparing you for the new times
That you may be firm in faith, and persevering in prayer,
So that the Holy Spirit may work through you,
And renew the face of the earth.

Mary's Message (in part) at Medjugorje on June 25, 2019,
the 38th Anniversary of the Apparitions

To the memory of Fr Vince Doyle [1935-2014],
co-founder of the Mary of the Angelus Community

Contents

Part Four—The Signs of Medjugorje 1981-2021

Author's Note

This book is a series of letters to Pope Francis written as I travelled on pilgrimage to the popular Marian healing shrines of Europe, returning to Medjugorje in Bosnia Herzegovina. The letters were written in English, translated to Spanish and posted in their countries of origin, with the exception of the last two letters, which were sent by FedEx courier from Australia. I received no replies to the letters—other than the attached letter from the office of the Secretary of State at the Vatican—and I have no idea whether the Pope read any of them.

While I am a practising Roman Catholic and generally subscribe to Church teaching, I wish to acknowledge that I could be wrong about my belief. Some people will be certain that there is no God, and all religion is a figment of human imagination. They could be right for all I know. The purpose of the pilgrimage was to examine the evidence for and against Marian apparitions, which the Church often describes as 'worthy of belief as private revelation'.

Whatever the truth about Marian apparitions, they are extraordinary phenomena, and not easily dismissed even after close examination. Perhaps Mary is a prophet of our times—the harbinger of what lies ahead. Like Pope Benedict XVI, I am inclined to believe that neither mankind nor the world can be saved unless God reappears in a convincing fashion.[1] Private revelations to six children (now adults) at

Medjugorje over the past 40 years may represent a significant foresight into what salvation for humanity and the Earth could look like.

SECRETARY OF STATE

FIRST SECTION - GENERAL MATTERS

Vatican City, January 9, 2021

Dear Mr Breen

Encouraged by feelings of filial attachment and affection, you were kind enough to write to the Holy Father, Pope Francis, and to make certain observations.

His Holiness appreciates this show of cordial closeness, and begs you to pray for him and for the fruits of his service to the Holy People of God. At the same time, he imparts to you from his heart the implored Apostolic Blessing, which he gladly extends to your family and other loved ones.

I take this opportunity to convey to you the testimony of my consideration and esteem in Christ.

Mons. L. Roberto Cona
Adviser

Peter BREEN
MULLUMBIMBY

Introductory Letter

Prodigal Pilgrim Group
Delivery Box #281
245 Eighth Avenue
New York, NY 10011
United States of America

June 25, 2019

Fr Jorge Mario Bergoglio
Holy Father Pope Francis
Papal Residence
Domus Sanctae Marthae
00120 Citta del Vaticano

Dear Fr Jorge

I write to introduce myself as I set out on pilgrimage to the four popular Marian apparition shrines of Europe. First stop is Lourdes in France, then Fatima in Portugal, followed by Garabandal in Spain, and finally, Medjugorje in Bosnia Herzegovina. Medjugorje is a shrine for the ages in my correspondence. Is it possible that a woman who lived on the Earth 2000 years ago—and now occupies some other dimension in time and space—has been visiting us daily for the past 40 years with the extraordinary, if unsurprising, revelation that God has the power to intervene in human affairs? In one of her first Medjugorje appearances in 1981, Mary the Mother of Jesus is credibly reported to have said to six young children: *You have forgotten that with prayer and fasting you can keep war at bay; you can suspend the laws of nature.*[2]

Please consider my correspondence as the reflections of a cautiously enthusiastic believer in Mary's apparitions, though one experiencing a crisis of faith in the Church. I was encouraged to write to you following a homily you gave a couple of months ago during your regular Sunday Angelus prayer service, when you asked the faithful to let you know how we think the Church might improve upon its mission to spread the Good News in the modern world. In the context of this generous request for feedback, I decided to put pen to paper, in the hope of giving you my perspective on the Marian apparitions. Already I can report—even before the start of my pilgrimage—that while my crisis of faith in the Church is widely shared, causing numbers attending Church services to drop off a cliff, devotion to Mary seems to be more popular than ever.

You will not be surprised to learn that my crisis of faith is a direct consequence of the sex abuse crimes committed against children in the care of the Church. A royal commission report into institutional responses to child sex abuse in Australia was particularly soul-destroying. Nearly 62 per cent of complaints to the commission involved Catholic perpetrators, yet Catholics are just 22 per cent of Australia's population. I feel shocked and deeply ashamed whenever I recall that the world's most senior cleric convicted of child sex abuse offences is Australia's George Cardinal Pell. One of the reasons for going on pilgrimage to my favorite Marian shrines is to take some time out to further consider the culpability of George the convict, a man I know personally and held in high esteem before his descent into hell as a child sex abuse offender. That said, I am aware that George may be innocent of the crimes for which he is convicted. An appeal has been lodged with the Court of Appeal, and if that fails, the cardinal will appeal to the High Court of Australia. I will write to you again when there is a final verdict.

As I write, George is serving a six years' prison sentence on the testimony of a credible witness who says the cardinal sexually assaulted him and another boy (now deceased) when they were child choristers at St Patrick's Cathedral in Melbourne in the mid-1990s. The initial appeal will be heard in the next couple of months. Lawyers acting for George the convict say that the testimony of the witness, though honestly given, is highly improbable in the light of 20 other 'opportunity witnesses' who described the movements of the cardinal in and around the cathedral at the time he was supposed to be committing the offences.

Some people say, triumphantly, that George's convictions and sentencing prove that the justice system works, and there is no need to be concerned about miscarriages of justice and unsafe or doubtful convictions. My experience of the legal system is rather less sanguine. Appeal courts are generally reluctant to interfere with jury decisions, which means most innocent prisoners never have the opportunity for a serious conviction review, as happened in the case of Lindy Chamber-lain who was jailed for the macabre murder in the desert of her baby, Azaria. The Northern Territory government of the day made a political decision to appeal the ruling of the coroner—that a dingo took the Chamberlain baby—because the coroner's finding reflected badly on police. Australian courts supported the police and overturned the coroner's decision. Lindy Chamberlain went to jail as a murderer, along with her husband Michael as an accessory after the fact. When all the legal remedies were exhausted, new, and exculpatory evidence in the form of Azaria's matinee jacket finally nailed the dingo. And still there are those who say that Lindy Chamberlain murdered her baby.

I should explain that this is not my first crisis of faith in the justice system or the Church. As a young man, I studied in a seminary with the intention of becoming a priest, until your predecessor, Pope Paul VI, ruled that birth control was sinful. That ruling was contrary to the recommendations of the Pontifical Commission on Birth Control, the advisory body established during Vatican Council II to consider the implications of contraception on Church moral teaching. Commission members recommended by 64 votes to five that the Church allow birth control. When it became obvious that the pope would not follow the majority recommendation of the council's commission, I could not remain in the seminary in good conscience, joining the 1960s exodus of student priests from religious life.

After about 20 years leave without pay from the Church, which included careers as a defense lawyer and politician, I found myself at the Marian shrine in Fatima trying to recall the fifteen decades of the rosary. Before I knew it, I was back in the fold with a new understanding of the primacy of conscience, and a passion for the modern private revelations of the Mother of Jesus—the Jewish woman in our camp, or 'Maryam' as she is known in the surahs of the Koran. As you know, some imams teach that Jesus, a son of Maryam and messenger of Allah, did not die but was raised to the presence of Allah. I do not know how that teaching sits with you, Holy Father, but it's not far from Christian teaching on the resurrection in my correspondence.

I moved to New York for a few months to resolve my most recent crisis of faith in the Church, since the Americans I know are much more sympathetic to religion than my mob Down Under. Historian Manning Clark described Australia as *a society unique in the history of mankind ... holding no firm beliefs on the existence of God or survival after death.*[3] Bear in mind that modern Australia was founded as an outpost of the British Empire—during the Enlightenment—when science and reason and belief in progress through dialogue began to overshadow tradition and religion. Overwhelmed by appalling injustice and the instinct to survive, convicts and colonists set up their governing institutions largely on the understanding that we are alone in the universe. Religion does not play an important part in the lives of most Australians according to author Donald Horne in his 1960s book *The*

Lucky Country—if there is a happy eternal life it's for everyone.

By way of contrast, 74 per cent of Americans today claim affiliation with a particular religious group—down from 84 per cent in 2007—according to statistics from the Pew Research Center. The United States was established by the Pilgrim Fathers and the Puritans as a refuge from religious conflict. America's founders wanted a belief system that resembled more closely the teaching of the Bible—they believed that both the Church of England and the Roman Church had become dogmatic and authoritarian. The founding fathers created the brave new world of a secular republic with a guarantee of religious freedom in the First Amendment to the US Constitution. In the Second Amendment, they enshrined the right to keep and bear arms—a right that evolved from England's bill of rights—to enable American states to protect themselves from the possibility of a tyrannical federal government. Some people say that gun laws are in place not to arm the militia—as the Supreme Court has ruled—but to protect citizens in the next civil war.

So here I am in New York—however temporarily—adjusting to a life where God and guns seem to rule the roost. Mind you, the way Americans politicize religion was a bit of a shock, as I prefer to see church and state kept well apart. Just the other day, the Billy Graham Evangelistic Association placed a full-page advertisement in the newspaper *USA Today* seeking divine intervention for the president. Readers were inveigled in bold print: *The only one who can fix our nation's problems is God Himself, and we pray that God will bless our President and our nation for His Glory.*[4] I don't mean to sound disrespectful, but Trump as God's man generally fails the pub test in Australia—as does the idea, by the way, that God will save us without any effort on our part to help each other.

I finally decided to make the journey to Europe following your decision last month to officially recognise pilgrimages to Medjugorje. It was a brave decision when there is so much resistance in the Church to the idea that Mary appears at Medjugorje. Having approved Medjugorje pilgrimages, you might consider taking the next step and proclaim the apparitions 'worthy of belief as private revelation'. Without your voice of approval, Holy Father, Mary's prophetic warnings are too easily dismissed as mass hysteria, delusion, or some form of magic.

Sincerely
Peter Breen
Prodigal Pilgrim Group

Part One

The Miracles of Lourdes 1858

Pilgrim Letter 1

A Meeting of Minds in the 'Holy Dip' Queue

Prodigal Pilgrim Group

Grand Hotel Moderne

21 Ave Bernadette Soubirous

Lourdes, France

June 30, 2019

Fr Jorge Mario Bergoglio

Holy Father Pope Francis

Papal Residence

Domus Sanctae Marthae

00120 Citta del Vaticano

Dear Fr Jorge

Flying time from New York's JFK airport to Paris-Orly airport was less than eight hours—a walk in the park when compared with the 30-odd hours it takes to fly from Australia. I felt rejuvenated upon arrival in the City of Love (or the City of Light if you prefer). Both titles seemed appropriate as I said goodbye to the woman seated next to me on the aircraft, a whip-smart American named Madeline who worked as an economist and investment adviser for an NGO in Paris. She flies into Paris from New York each Monday and flies out again on Friday.

Christian by birth and skeptical by nature, Madeline thought that the prospect of earthly visitations by the Mother of Jesus was a bit over the top—if God is about, he or she is unlikely to sanction flitting in and out of temporal existence. Not so long ago, I observed, commuting back and forth from the US to Europe by aircraft was inconceivable. I promised to call her—even if I found nothing new under the Medjugorje sun.

An hour later, I boarded an aircraft for the 80 minutes flight to the Tarbes-Lourdes airport, where I joined a shuttle bus for the city of Lourdes in the foothills of the Pyrenees. Checking into the Grand Hotel Moderne—the hotel in closest proximity to the world's most famous healing shrine—the concierge introduced me to a dapper Frenchman, Ulpiano, the guide for the tour group I would be accompanying for the next few days in Lourdes. Early in the evening, I caught up with Ulpiano and my fellow travelers, who invited me to join them on a stroll across the forecourt of the two basilicas in the precinct of the Massabielle grotto, where 'the Lady' appeared to 14-year-old Bernadette Soubirous in 1858. At the end of the short walk, I declined a further invitation to attend the nightly Lourdes candlelight procession, preferring instead the comfort and solitude of my hotel room—and an early night.

Ulpiano and I were the first of the group to foregather next morning outside the hotel. The tour guide was a dead ringer for Agatha Christie's Inspector Poirot with his inquisitive eyebrows and splendid moustache. He said that the

Church officially approved the Lourdes apparitions in 1862, after several miraculous cures at the grotto in response to pilgrims' prayers seeking God's healing power through the intercession of 'the Lady'. Since the Church approved the apparitions, the Lourdes Medical Bureau had documented about 7,000 healings, although the Church in its wisdom officially sanctioned just 70 of these cures. I would put Lourdes on my bucket list of papal pilgrimages if I were you, Holy Father. With six million visitors to the city each year (about 100,000 of them estimated to be seriously ill), Lourdes is the second most popular tourist destination in France after Paris.

I learned that Lourdes is named after a local Muslim leader who surrendered the city peacefully to Charlemagne in 778 CE. And Ulpiano updated the pilgrim group on Lourdes history, telling us that Bernadette was attending to wounded soldiers in the St Gildard Convent at Nevers when France was at war with the Prussian Empire in the early 1870s. One of the nuns admonished the young visionary for looking after enemy soldiers. Bernadette replied that God is in the heart of the enemy, no less than in the hearts of French soldiers.

It was Ulpiano who first drew my attention to the expression the 'holy dip' to describe the Lourdes healing baths, located some 60 yards past the Massabielle grotto, along the flagstone pavement that separates the base of the mountain from the Gave River. Initially, I assumed the Frenchman was referring to pilgrims in general with the words 'holy trip', until one of the bemused Americans put me on the right track. Ulpiano was saying that the men's queue for the 'holy dip' healing baths moved faster than the women's queue, for reasons he did not fully understand. The simple explanation for the faster queue is that the male section of the baths had less regard for privacy than the female section, crowding half a dozen men into a holding cell for undressing. Women had their own private undressing rooms—I know that now after comparing notes with two women pilgrims who took the plunge.

I decided to join the men's queue for a 'holy dip' after parting company with Ulpiano. But first I would like to place in context Mary's modern appearances on Earth and go back to the beginning of the Lourdes apparitions. As you know, 'the Lady' first appeared to Bernadette on February 11, 1858, while she was gathering firewood with two friends at the edge of what was then the village of Lourdes. The child was between the Gave River and the Massabielle grotto when the apparition appeared. *I looked up and saw a cluster of branches and brambles underneath the topmost opening in the grotto [where I saw] a girl in white, no bigger than myself, who greeted me with a slight bow of the head; at the same time, she stretched out her arms away from her body, opening her hands as in pictures of Our Lady.*[5]

During the third of the 18 apparitions at the Lourdes grotto—at the request of one of the spectators—Bernadette handed up pencil and paper and asked the apparition to write down her name. Bernadette said that the young girl appearing before her in the grotto began to laugh, and then spoke for the first time saying *There is no need to write down what I have to say.* [6] From then on, Bernadette referred to the visitor as 'the Lady'. When questioned by the Lourdes police investigator, Bernadette said 'the Lady' appeared *as if standing in a soft light.* In response to further questions the visionary said, *I cannot explain these things to you [but] what I can assure you of is that she is real and alive, that she moves, smiles, and speaks just like us.* [7]

On February 25, 1858, 'the Lady' appeared to the visionary for the ninth time. An eyewitness, Elfrida Lacrampe—a local woman and one of about 500 spectators—described Bernadette kneeling on the ground outside the grotto and praying the rosary while communicating in a state of ecstasy with 'the Lady'. *The child had not recited a decade of her beads when suddenly she set off on her knees and began to clamber in this way up the slope that led to the interior of the grotto.* [8]

Bernadette said later that she was following instructions. *The Lady said to me: 'Go and drink at the spring and wash yourself in it.' Not seeing any spring [in the grotto] I was going to drink from the Gave.* Apparently at the apparition's direction, the child—still on her knees—found her way to the back of the grotto and dug in the ground with her fingers. *I saw merely a bit of dirty water; I put my hand in it, but could not get hold of any. I scratched and the water came, but muddy. Three times I threw it away; the fourth time I was able to drink some.* [9]

One of her aunts, Bernarde Casterot—a widow of modest means who owned a tavern—helped walk Bernadette down from the slope, wiping the child's face and mouth, and later telling investigators: *The ecstasy over, we took her back. People were jeering. We walked quickly along the road to escape the crowd. They were following us as though it were a comedy.* Some people in the crowd were calling out that Bernadette was mad. The same aunt reported Bernadette's movements during a previous apparition, saying the child *bows and smiles [during the ecstasy], and from time to time [there is] a small movement of the lips ... To see her face like that, brought tears to your eyes.*[10] Meanwhile the pool of muddy water was expanding. Within days it was a steady stream flowing out of the grotto. A decade later, the source of the water was found to be a spring in the Massabielle limestone.

Remarkable healings attributed to washing, drinking, and bathing in the clear water began within days: a quarryman, Louis Bouriette, blind in one eye from a mine explosion and suffering from an incurable amaurosis, had his sight restored; a child named Julien, dying of progressive paralysis, and bathed by his mother in the spring water, walked for the first time. Doctors who had given the boy just days to live determined he was fully recovered, with no medical explanation.

News of the healings spread through Southern France— nearly 10,000 people descended on the grotto for the 15th apparition on March 4, 1858. Cure Abbe Peyramale, the parish priest of Lourdes, again directed Bernadette to ask 'the Lady' her name. Bernadette did as she was told, reporting that 'the Lady' just smiled in answer to the question. During the 16th apparition on March 25, 1858, the Church's feast day of the Annunciation, Bernadette asked 'the Lady' three times to disclose her name, and finally she obliged. Immediately following the apparition, Bernadette was heard repeating the answer, which she did not understand. *I am the Immaculate Conception.*[11] This eponymous name and title for Mary, declared a dogma of faith by your predecessor, Pope Pius IX, just four years earlier in 1854, assured the veracity of the apparitions in my opinion, since the child visionary had no way of being informed in March 1858 about a description of Mary in those words.

Bernadette observed the serendipitous confluence between the name of 'the Lady' and papal authority in a letter to Pope Pius IX, written at the request of her local bishop in December 1876. *I did not know what that ['I am the Immaculate Conception'] meant; I had never heard [those words]. But since then, whenever I ponder the matter, I say to myself: How good the Blessed Virgin is! One would think she came to confirm the words of Our Holy Father.*[12] The letter was written when the visionary was a nun at the Nevers convent, and it's generally agreed that her superiors had a hand in revising the letter. Even so, it seems unlikely that the most famous visionary in recent Marian history would allow her testimony to be compromised by editors changing the meaning of her words. It's uncontested in my correspondence that the dogma of Mary's conception without the stain of original sin was confirmed at Lourdes.

Informed consciences will differ on the other obvious question—whether papal infallibility was reinforced by the apparitions at Lourdes. Of much greater interest to my mind is what the Church will do to validate Marian apparitions in the light of the overriding Christian principle that all public revelation of Jesus ended with the death of the last apostle. It may be a long bow to draw, but given that Mary was a contemporary of Jesus' apostles, there is a reasonable argument that the Church could recognise another category of public revelation beyond the limited references to Mary in Scripture. I will say something more about public and private revelation, if I may, in another letter.

By the late 1870s, Bernadette was mostly confined to the convent's infirmary, in what she described as a *habitual state of suffering*.[13] She suffered from a large tumor on the right knee, bone decay, anemia and chest ailments related to her lifelong asthma condition, as well as endless spiritual attack. She died in the infirmary aged 35 years on April 16, 1879, and her body was interred in a lead-lined casket in the convent's chapel. Some 30 years later, the local bishop ordered the exhumation of the body as part of the cause for the young visionary's canonization, and the body was found to be incorrupt. The crucifix and rosary beads buried with her were tarnished and rusted, but the flesh of her body remained intact—there was no trace of odor or decomposition. As you may have seen for yourself, Holy Father, Bernadette's incorrupt body remains on display to this day in a crystal reliquary in the chapel.

On December 8, 1933—the feast day of the Immaculate Conception—50,000 witnesses, including surviving members of the Soubirous family, crowded into St Peter's Basilica to hear Pope Pius XI announce that the name of Bernadette Soubirous had been added to the roll of saints. He described Bernadette as a simple miller's daughter who bore witness to the revelations of Mary, passing on her messages including her exhortations to penance which *procured for the world the magnificent spectacle of Lourdes, its three sanctuaries, its pilgrimages, its graces of conversion, of calls to perfection and of miraculous cures.*[14]

All this, Holy Father, leads me back to the 'holy dip' queue, which these days consists of a couple of dozen long benches not unlike Church pews—half for the women's section and half for the men. The sick and infirm wait patiently, sitting in wheelchairs and laying on mobile hospital beds alongside the benches. As people wait, attendants gradually move those at the head of the queue through a vertically striped blue and white curtain at the entrance to the bathing compartments, or 'piscines' as they are called in French.

Things became difficult in the male queue when the Italian bloke seated to my right decided I needed to move more quickly as the queue progressed. There he was, looking over my shoulder at the gap between me and the bloke ahead of me, and getting in my ear with his repetitive 'Andiamo!' ('Let's go!'). The more he urged me on, the slower I moved, causing the gap in the queue to become wider. Instead of just moving aside for the Italian—doing the humble and sensible thing—I was torn between trying to recall the words of the healing prayer for sinful anger, and headbutting the guy in a meeting of minds.

Any chance of a healing was lost by the time our section of the queue was ushered through the blue and white striped curtain. Six of us —now at the head of the queue—were directed into one of the holding cells and told in French to strip down to our underwear. Unhappily, I was in the confined space with the Italian, who was still whining about the queue, even as he sat in the naughty corner in his y-fronts. Suddenly two attendants took me by each arm, ushered me through another curtain and directed me to drop my undies. Then they wrapped me in a damp towel, prayed over me in French and dunked me in the holy piscine, which was so cold I let out a yelp like a startled puppy dog.

Emerging cold and dripping wet from the bathing compartment, I managed to dry myself with the wet towel, dressed, and found my way outside, where I leaned on the stone wall that overlooks the fast-flowing Gave river. Warming myself in the morning sun, I was soon regretting the lost opportunity to do something about my sinful anger.

Sincerely
Peter Breen
Prodigal Pilgrim Group

Pilgrim Letter 2
Something Each Way in a Divided Church

Prodigal Pilgrim Group
Grand Hotel Moderne
21 Ave Bernadette Soubirous
Lourdes, France

July 6, 2019

Fr Jorge Mario Bergoglio
Holy Father Pope Francis
Papal Residence
Domus Sanctae Marthae
00120 Citta del Vaticano

Dear Fr Jorge

I counted about 30 pilgrims in the Lourdes tour group, most of whom identified themselves as belonging to one of two political camps—the Trump lovers and the Trump haters—which roughly lined up with their conservative and progressive religious affiliations. The hot button issue for the pilgrims was abortion. An American Dominican priest and spiritual director with the pilgrimage, Fr Ben form Colorado, informed me that wealthy organizations and individuals donated to the Trump campaign for president in 2016 because Trump was the only candidate committed to appointing conservative Supreme Court judges who might overturn *Roe v Wade.* And yet just 28 per cent of Americans are convinced that completely scrapping the decision is a good idea according to new figures from the Pew Research Center. [15]

Of all the candidates for president in 2016, Trump was arguably the least interested in abortion per se, even though he championed abortion law reform for the election funding it represented. Other candidates took a leaf out of your book, Holy Father, believing that equally sacred as the innocent unborn *are the lives of the poor, those already born, the destitute, the abandoned and the underprivileged, the vulnerable infirm and elderly exposed to covert euthanasia, the victims of human trafficking, new forms of slavery, and every form of rejection.* [16] The important point you made, I think, is that people of goodwill recognize and respect the dignity of human life in all its complex forms.

A couple of nights ago, about a dozen pilgrims and their friends randomly sat down for dinner at a large circular table in the Lourdes' hotel dining room. I sat next to a young ex-military man named Mike who was wearing a red 'Make America Great Again' baseball cap. To my left was a young woman named Mary-Ann from upstate New York who had complained to me earlier that her local priest was not a real priest—he had been incardinated in her local diocese only after being granted an annulment of his marriage. Across the table, the Dominican priest was saying that you are in trouble for trying to change some words of the Lord's Prayer. Instead of the words *Lead us not into temptation,* you are apparently wanting to say *Do not allow us to be led into temptation.* Common sense suggested the change was long overdue.

I had already engaged with Fr Ben on the question whether the interpretation of Scripture was set in concrete. For this reason, I stayed out of the discussion about the words of the Lord's Prayer, deferring to the priest's authority even as I strained across the table to listen to what was being said. An older man insisted that the pope had no right to change the Lord's Prayer. His wife disagreed, assuring those of us at the table who had her attention that popes have investigated the possibility of updating the Lord's prayer for 50 years. It just so happened that the decision is apparently being made on your watch. It fell to the priest at the table to repeat his observation that there will be trouble if you change the words—and that was pretty much the end of the discussion.

I liked this priest who fiercely defended the Church and doubted that the faithful could sustain opinions that contradict Church teaching on faith and morals—even though we do. He was sure George Pell was innocent and I hoped he was right. Following our discussion about the Pell case, Fr Ben sent me regular press clippings by email, all of which argued that George was in the wrong place at the wrong time. I told him I had acted for several innocent convicts over the years—most of whom were the victims of over-exuberant policing—and I regretted that Australia had no criminal cases review commission to re-examine unsafe convictions. If George's appeals failed he was up the pro-verbial creek.

Mike in the red MAGA cap was chatting to an Englishman with a Geordie accent—one of the pilgrim's friends who had joined us for dinner. I heard Mike say that according to the Catechism of the Catholic Church, the fetus is a person from the moment of conception. I took the liberty of interjecting myself, saying the Catechism says the fetus has the rights of a person, not that it's a person. This response delighted the Geordie who was emboldened to ask Mike to take off his MAGA hat during dinner. After a fleeting moment of tension at the table, Mike did as he was asked and removed the red cap, to reveal a shaved bald head, which prompted the Geordie to say that he liked Donald Trump's hair. I held my breath as a wry smile slipped out of Mike's mouth.

Later in the evening, Mike and I were alone at the table, talking about the radically different rules about gun ownership in Australia and the USA. I was asking what I thought were innocuous questions about the types of guns you could buy in America, and I was surprised to hear the young man describe in graphic detail how a terrorist might shoot up the hotel's restaurant—beginning with the people at the bar which was close to the exit door. As the bodies piled up, he continued, you could probably 'pop' everyone with a couple of semi-automatic rifles and a handgun or two. I changed the subject to America's Independence Day which we had celebrated earlier in the week. Did he know that Australia was still constitutionally joined at the hip to the British monarchy?

As I headed up the sweeping wooden staircase for the night to my hotel room on the second floor, I wondered how it would ever be possible to reconcile all the conflicting views in the Church. Even at the peak of summer, Lourdes is cool at night, and a soft breeze entered my room when I opened the French doors that separated the room from the balcony. The five-story hotel was built in the late 1890s in the French classic style of the day with Juliet balconies abutted by fluted stone columns and gargoyles. Leaning on the balcony's wrought iron railing, I watched the people milling about in the street below, and across the Lourdes sanctuary, the flickering candlelight procession intersected with the stars of a cloudless night sky.

The number and diversity of people who participate in the nightly procession at Lourdes caused me to think about the origins of the Church at the First Pentecost when thousands of Jewish people from different countries had traveled to Jerusalem to celebrate seven weeks after Passover. Filled with the Holy Spirit, the Apostle Peter *burst forth from the upper room and addressed them; miraculously, all these Jews, with their various languages, clearly understood what Peter was saying.*[17] Some people in the crowd believed Peter was merely babbling like a drunkard; others insisted that the apostles had power from the Spirit to exercise all the spiritual gifts, including physical healing and the ability to speak in different tongues. Like many Christians today, I look forward to a Second Pentecost, when the Holy Spirit enables us, once again, to communicate in a language that everybody understands.

During the feast of Pentecost this year you hosted charismatic groups in Rome for their annual pilgrimage to the Eternal City, encouraging them to remain connected to the broader Church. I was delighted to hear you say that as many as 100 million Catholics regard themselves as charismatic Christians. You might have mentioned that more than a quarter of the world's two billion Christians are charismatic, according to the Pew Research Center.[18] You counselled charismatics against fear of change, saying this kind of thinking did not come from the Spirit—perhaps from the spirit of the world but not from the Holy Spirit.[19] With respect, I do not think charismatic Christians fear change so much as they fear the confusion caused by Christian disunity.

I know you will not mind me telling you how to do your job—this must be true otherwise you would not have asked for feedback—but you were on the right track last month when you described the charismatic movement as *'a current of the grace of the Holy Spirit' being poured out for the renewal of the church in our time.*[20] May I conclude by saying that the charismatic movement offers a wonderful opportunity for you, Holy Father, to call on all Christians to get together and speak with one voice. A unified Church was one of the ambitions of the Second Vatican Ecumenical Council, as contemplated in the *Decree on Ecumenism* which speaks of *a movement, fostered by the grace of the Holy Spirit, for the restoration of unity among all Christians.*[21]

Sincerely
Peter Breen
Prodigal Pilgrim Group

Pilgrim Letter 3

Conscience as a Lifeline to Cautious Faith

Prodigal Pilgrim Group

Grand Hotel Moderne

21 Ave Bernadette Soubirous

Lourdes, France

July 14, 2019

Fr Jorge Mario Bergoglio

Holy Father Pope Francis

Papal Residence

Domus Sanctae Marthae

00120 Citta del Vaticano

Dear Fr Jorge

I trust that my letter finds you well and in good spirits. These past few days of peace and quiet at Lourdes have allowed me to consider, once again, the question whether a person can participate in the life of the Church without signing up for teachings at odds with their conscience. It's a struggle I seem to return to from time to time and never quite resolve. I suspect the reflection was prompted by the Dominican priest opposing changes to the Lord's prayer and the woman from upstate New York raising concerns about the efficacy of priestly ordination following marriage annulment. While the Church teaches that a person *has the right to act in conscience and in freedom so as personally to make moral decisions,*[22] constantly being at odds with the Church does cause anxiety and doubt about the veracity of Church teaching more generally. Often I wonder whether I have all the facts, or perhaps I am wrong about the facts I think I have.

At other times, I take comfort in the foundational arguments of another Dominican priest, St Thomas Aquinas, who said in the 13th century that any victim of unjust ecclesiastical authority *should perish in excommunication rather than violate his [or her] conscience.*[23] You will recall that Australia's first canonized saint, the Josephite nun Mary MacKillop, was excommunicated for around six months in 1871 for alleged insubordination. More recently, there is loose talk in the ranks of some Catholic bishops who want to excommunicate certain politicians for failing to toe the line on abortion. Other bishops are to be sacked for ordaining women priests. It's an even money bet, Holy Father, which bishops will one day be added to the roll of saints.

Consistent with divisions among the bishops, the pilgrims I have met at Lourdes are at odds with the Church over one thing or another—some of us seem to have a shopping list of grievances—but we remain committed to the Church *assisted by the gifts of the Holy Spirit, aided by the witness or advice from others and guided by the authoritative teaching.*[24] Included in my list of authoritative teachings is the *Declaration on Religious Freedom* first published by the Second Vatican Ecumenical Council in 1965. In all their activities, a person is bound to follow their conscience in order that they *may come to God, the end and purpose of life. It follows that [they] are not to be forced to act in a manner contrary to [their] conscience.*[25]

In Australia—already the most culturally diverse country in the world—we have the benefit of an extra layer of diversity in the clergy with priests from India, Nigeria, Kenya and the Philippines serving the people in my local diocese—priests who have an understanding of their faith that is necessarily influenced by their history and culture. To a man, these peregrine priests have a humble and compassionate approach to Church teaching—moderated perhaps by indigenous lore and practice—which sometimes causes scandal among their ageing antipodean contemporaries. It makes me smile to think that these saintly foreigners propping up the male priesthood in Australia are the fruits of western missionaries who colonized their ancestors.

Add to that mix numerous priests from the Anglican and Episcopal communions who have been ordained as Catholic priests in recent years. Many of them bring their wives and children to the new job, which I reckon is a fabulous development in the life of the Church. I might get a guernsey myself as a priest in this modern evangelization of the Church but for my advancing years—*running out of runway* to quote my wife, Diane Thomas. It may not happen in my lifetime, but it's not difficult to foresee a time when women are ordained deacons, and eventually priests, in numbers equivalent to men; a time when nobody questions the sexual identity of priests who choose not to have partners; and a time when those who do have the consolation of a partner are no longer harangued about their relationship proclivities and whether they can be trusted with children.

I hope you are still with me at this point since there is something more to be said about choosing according to conscience, and it relates directly to my pilgrimage to Lourdes. When I left New York, I was a supporter of a woman's right to choose an abortion in all cases—regardless of how she became pregnant, the stage of her pregnancy or Church teaching on the viability of human life. During the flight from JFK airport to Paris, I could not argue with Madeline seated next to me on the aircraft, who assured me that one in four pregnancies end in abortion or miscarriage, and the natural mortality rate for human embryos (fertilized eggs) may be as high as 70 per cent.

In fact, I had always supported a woman's right to choose based on human rights principles, and I was a harsh critic of Latin America's restrictive abortion laws. The American Convention on Human Rights is an international treaty that seeks to establish a secular rule that the fetus is a person and that life should be protected from the moment of conception. Although the convention is consistent with Church teaching, every other relevant human rights instrument in the world—to my knowledge—suggests that the fetus is not a person until birth, and the fetus has no rights in human rights law independent of the mother.

Even so, I find myself reconsidering my understanding of abortion law on this pilgrimage, in the light of Mary's affirmation of the Immaculate Conception doctrine. If Mary was conceived without sin on her own testimony, validating the concept of original sin, it must follow that life in some form exists from the moment of conception for the purpose of abortion law—as the Church has always taught—and that the Church is correct when it says *we cannot tamper with the revelation of original sin without undermining the mystery of Christ.*[26]

Assuming life exists from the moment of conception, does it follow that all forms of human life are the same? And if I do not agree in good conscience with Church moral teaching on abortion, or with politicizing religious beliefs more generally, does that mean I am no longer permitted to participate in the life of the Church? Or is it the case that I am entitled to continue practicing my faith in good conscience but with the usual caveats—an informed conscience and an open mind? A paragraph of questions, Holy Father.

There is a world of difference in the way Australians approach abortion law reform compared to the approach taken by the people of the United States. It seems that 80 per cent of Australians believe that a woman should have the right to choose an abortion—except in the last trimester, when support for the right to choose drops to 48 per cent. A 2007 poll by the Australian Survey of Social Attitudes found that just 4 per cent of the Australian population opposed abortion in all circumstances. Consistent with these figures, Australian law provides for safe access zones to protect the rights of women, making it a criminal offence to conduct an abortion protest within 150 yards of an abortion clinic. Catholic politicians going into bat for the Church on abortion law reform can easily find themselves in serious trouble with a significant majority of their constituents unless they make it clear that their remarks are directed to those who profess to be Christians.

So, how do I reconcile the Church's teaching that life begins at conception (as affirmed by Mary at Lourdes) with my conscience, which tells me that in any conflict between the rights of the fetus and the rights of the mother, the first consideration must be the mother's rights? In his book *Acting on Conscience*, Jesuit priest Frank Brennan makes the point that, for most people, *disposing of a beaker full of embryos is not the moral equivalent of committing thousands of partial-birth abortions on near-viable fetuses.*[27] My fellow airline passenger commuting from New York to Paris made the same point.

The viability of the fetus is on a continuum from the moment of conception to the moment of birth, and different rules apply along the way in my correspondence. More than half the embryos naturally produced in the womb fail to develop beyond a couple of cells. Correct me if I am wrong, but there is no infallible papal declaration on abortion. While Pope John Paul II insisted that abortion *always constitutes a grave moral disorder*, his successor and your immediate predecessor, Pope Benedict XVI, doubted that the words were spoken infallibly.[28] Benedict followed the approach of John Henry Newman, *noting that Newman embraced 'a papacy not put in opposition to the primacy of conscience but based on it and guaranteeing it'.*[29]

Newman appears on your list of prospective saints to be canonized later in the year, so it might be opportune to remind the faithful that the saintly Englishman famously said that he would happily toast the infallibility of the pope, but *to Conscience first, and to the Pope afterwards.*[30] In other words, there can be no conflict, since conscience must always prevail over papal pronouncements. My understanding is that the pope cannot speak infallibly without first checking to ensure that the proposed doctrine is, in fact, a truth held by the faithful.

Some of us feel like Galileo must have felt when the Inquisition decided that the Earth and not the Sun was at the center of the known universe. Yes, Pope John Paul II apologized to Galileo nearly 400 years down the track, but I do not think we have that long to cavil at the Church's misadventures. The same pope apologized for more recent wrongheadedness in the Church: the African slave trade; the Church's involvement in Australia's stolen generations of Aboriginal people; the silence of Catholics during the Holocaust; violation of women's rights, especially legal equality; and most recently, the sexual abuse of children in the care of the Church. Like Galileo, I mutter away about problems with the lenses the Church is looking through, even as I agonize over the possibility that dissent may be a more egregious problem than grudging compliance.

Nobody wants conflict with the people and organizations they love, tolerating even fundamental differences for the greater good. But fundamental differences are corrosive, eating away at relationships until one party or the other walks away. Inevitably, the greater good becomes personal integrity and survival. Help me with this, Holy Father—the torment of the contradictor. Is it trite to ask a question on notice: whether love—the greatest of the Holy Spirit's gifts and the only universal gift—conquers all dissent and division?

Galileo did the wise thing, recanting in time to save his skin from the Inquisition. Many of us today do the same, avoiding disapprobation by deferring to the insistent voices demanding adherence to Church teaching on faith and morals. The doggedly faithful tell me I can leave if I do not like the rules, but it's not so easy if you still have a cautious faith—if you are not ready to join the *I don't believe that stuff anymore* mob. Besides, the real test of a person's faith is whether they subscribe to the hard truths: the divinity of Jesus, his death, bodily resurrection, and ascension; the Church sacraments; the communion of saints; the choirs of angels; and the promise of merciful judgment and salvation for all people of goodwill. The practical reality may be that the moral questions, at least, pale to insignificance alongside the hard truths.

According to your immediate predecessor, Pope Benedict XVI, true respect for the dignity of the human person means conscience is *the meeting point and common ground of Christians and non-Christians and consequently [is] the real hinge on which dialogue turns.*[31] Cautious faith demands a free and open mind on questions of faith and morals, ensuring people outside the tent are not excluded from the salvation dialogue. As Frank Brennan says at the end of his book on the primacy of conscience: we can be religious people without renouncing our moral and mental freedom, especially if we hope to communicate with people of other faiths and of no faith.

In closing, I was delighted last month to see you on the television news celebrating the feast of the Immaculate Heart of Mary at the replica of the Lourdes grotto in the Vatican Gardens. I was there in the gardens a few years

ago—quite near the built Massabielle grotto—when I en-
countered the then Russian president, Mikhail Gorbachev. I
look forward to telling you more about that experience
when the pilgrimage takes me to Portugal and the shrine of
Our Lady of Fatima.

Sincerely
Peter Breen
Prodigal Pilgrim Group

Pilgrim Letter 4

In Search of Revelation through 'the Lady'

Prodigal Pilgrim Group

Grand Hotel Moderne

21 Ave Bernadette Soubirous

Lourdes, France

July 18, 2019

Fr Jorge Mario Bergoglio

Holy Father Pope Francis

Papal Residence

Domus Sanctae Marthae

00120 Citta del Vaticano

Dear Fr Jorge

I arrived early for morning Mass at the Massabielle grotto with the American pilgrims—so early that we shared the last of the cold night air and the mists that drifted across the grotto precinct from the banks of the Gave river. Seated in the open-air pews facing the makeshift altar in front of the grotto, waiting for the first rays of the morning sun to kickstart one of our last days at Lourdes, I spoke to an Illinois man who had travelled on pilgrimage to the healing shrine with his wife and two daughters. I asked him what he thought of the 'holy dip'. Like me, he had mixed feelings, but then he recalled that pilgrims who fail to receive a physical healing at the shrine will often receive a spiritual healing or insight instead—a consolation cure, if you like, Holy Father.

I could see no reason why the Holy Spirit's gift of knowledge would not be available at Lourdes as a consolation for pilgrims. Lourdes taught me about the spiritual dynamic between 'the Lady' and the Holy Spirit—the Church draws a clear distinction between 'devotion' to Mary and 'adoration' of God in the Father, the Son, and the Holy Spirit.[32] Even so, many religious people have a deep affection for Mary as the mother of Jesus—the God-man *who was conceived by the Holy Spirit*[33]—an affection developed through praying the rosary and reflecting on the role of Mary in salvation.

Auschwitz victim, St Maximilian Kolbe, took a pragmatic approach to the charge of 'Mariolatry' sometimes levelled against believers seeking out Mary to intercede or mediate with God on their behalf. *If anyone wishes to contact a President, for instance, or some other high worldly dignitary, he does not go about it by himself; he takes an intermediary with him. The same thing is true when we approach God; let it always be with Mary and through Mary.*[34] Maximilian Kolbe believed that Mary's whole being was so endowed with the gifts of the Holy Spirit that not only was she uniquely free of sin, but she had a place in human history and destiny like no other. She moves effortlessly through time and space, between this world and the next, appears in different places at the same time through the gift of bilocation, converses with people of different nationalities in their native tongue—both in their own language and their local dialect—and, most importantly for this generation, she has the gift of prophecy in spades.

Mary's prophecies for our time began at Rue de Bac in Paris in 1830, when she appeared in apparition and asked that a medal be struck to commemorate her being conceived without sin. The visionary was the convent postulant, St Catherine Laboure, who followed the instructions of the apparition which included the detail for both sides of the medal. It became known as the Immaculate Conception medal or 'Miraculous Medal' because of the extraordinary number of physical and spiritual healings attributed to wearing or carrying the medal as a sacramental. *No sacramental of the Church had such an impact as the Miraculous Medal did on the Catholic world since the Rosary was said to have routed the Albigensians in the 13th century.*[35] Like Bernadette Soubirous at Lourdes, Catherine Laboure's body was disinterred after being buried for 57 years and found to be incorrupt. According to the author John Haffert, the importance of Catherine Laboure is that the saintly nun gave us the first prophecy of the Marian Age almost two hundred years ago. *O how wonderful it will be to hear Mary as*

Queen of the World ... it will be a time of peace, joy and prosperity that will last long.[36]

At La Salette in the French Alps, Mary again appeared to two children in 1846, giving them separate prophecies in the form of secrets about the future. At the direction of their bishop, the children wrote down their secrets and placed them in sealed envelopes which were opened by your predecessor, Pope Pius IX, in 1851—the same year the Church gave formal approval to the La Salette apparition. You will recall that the resealed envelopes and their contents were discovered in the archives of the Congregation for the Doctrine of the Faith in 1999. They were the subject of a doctoral thesis at the Angelicum and a book.

You do not need me to tell you, Holy Father, that the time for the catastrophes predicted at La Salette has long passed; or alternatively, they were fulfilled in the two world wars of the 20th century. One curious La Salette prophecy— that all nations will convert after the troubles—seems like a bridge too far for some people, but the prophecy is consistent with other Marian forewarnings. Perhaps the most intriguing aspect of La Salette is the precision of the words given to an uneducated child of 11 years, Maximin Giraud, to the effect that a European country would be converted and *by the support of this country all the other nations of the world will be converted. Before all that arrives, great disorders will arrive, in the Church, and elsewhere.*[37]

Even at Lourdes, 'the Lady' gave Bernadette secrets in the form of prophecies which the seer took to her grave, although it's generally agreed that they related to Bernadette's personal life and not to the fate of the rest of us—unlike the prophecies of Fatima, Garabandal and Medjugorje, which are said to have worldwide implications. But I do not want to get ahead of myself, Holy Father. Suffice to say at this stage that the modern European prophecies of 'the Lady' do have as a common theme—upheaval and dislocation followed by a period of peace in which Mary Immaculate will triumph over evil.

Given the extent of her prophetic gifts of the Holy Spirit, Mary is arguably the greatest prophet in human history. I wonder what you think of that proposition, in the light of her latest prophecies at Medjugorje? I hasten to add that I am not talking end times or the Parousia—events beyond my pay grade—but rather the idea of a period of peace in the world, with everybody enjoying the gifts of the Holy Spirit. It's an alluring prospect in my correspondence, consistent with biblical revelation of a thousand years of peace. Another alluring prospect is the idea of further divine revelation, an idea worthy of more serious theological attention than you might think, Holy Father. I read the book *Militant Grace* by Canadian theologian Philip Zeigler, which gave me a new understanding of the word 'apocalyptic' to mean a 'revealing', which is consistent with the original Greek meaning of the word. Putting aside for one moment the

Protestant and Catholic thing about Mary, it would not be beyond the realms of possibility for God to act through the woman filled with the Holy Spirit to announce *a divine incursion from without, the invasion of divine grace*?[38]

Many of my friends—tribal believers, I suppose—flatly reject the idea of God intervening in human history. Never mind the idea of further divine revelation ending with the New Testament—the tribal mob would say that God decided to butt out after the Big Bang, and we have been on our own since at least the slime pool days. All appeals to an immanent God—whether by individuals, communities, armies, nations, or empires—fall on deaf ears. If God is about, she should show herself.

Of course, my friends in the Mary of the Angelus Community see God everywhere and in everything. I drifted away from the charismatic prayer group after it was founded in the 1990s, although I have been more involved since the organization received official approval as a Church lay association in 2013. A young priest with a good knowledge of the gifts of the Holy Spirit recently joined the group, so I asked this new priest about his take on private and public revelation, and the idea of further divine revelation, based on the original meaning of 'apocalyptic' as a 'revealing'. He asked the obvious question—whether this new Protestant theology included Mary's prophetic messages—and when I said no, he was skeptical. Nevertheless, the priest did volunteer an eschatological overview of what he believes is happening in the world, and it's one you may find interesting, Holy Father.

A tall man with dark curly hair, Fr Emil Milat's Croatian parents moved to Australia in 1960 from a refugee camp in the Italian port city of Trieste, in the top corner of the Adriatic Sea opposite Venice. Emil was born in Melbourne in the late 1960s. After graduating from the Australian National University in Canberra with degrees in commerce and law, he attended a seminary for secular priests at Kensington in Sydney. Today he is the parish priest in the Canberra suburbs of Braddon and Dickson. When I first visited Fr Emil at Braddon, he was praying in the back of the church, and I asked a local parishioner—a pious woman tidying the church after Mass—if she thought it would be alright for me to disturb the priest in his prayer. *That would be like waking the dead* said the woman. Many people regard Fr Emil as a holy man with a big-picture view of the Church in the modern world.

Over lunch in the presbytery, the priest reminded me that the Judeo-Christian faith is marked by three distinct eras. The first era began with the prophet Elijah, who encouraged the people of Israel in the ninth century BCE to recognize and worship the monotheistic 'Yahweh' or 'God the Father', instead of their worldly gods. In the second era, the prophet John the Baptist announced the revolutionary and redemptive 'God the Son', Jesus Christ. In the third era, Mary as prophet exemplar prepares us for the era of 'God the Holy Spirit', in which the gifts and fruits of the Spirit will be fully manifest in all people of goodwill. Christians have prayed the words of the Lord's Prayer for two millennia for God's kingdom to come on Earth, and to be filled with the fire of God's love in a new Pentecost—a new outpouring of the Holy Spirit.

Down through the ages of Christian history, the direct experience of the presence of Jesus Christ has faded, so in turn the influence of the Holy Spirit has diminished, until it appears again to renew the face of the Earth in the new era heralded by modern Marian apparitions. I wanted to know from the new priest whether those of us in two minds about the Church's moral teaching could expect any comfort from 'the Comforter' (the name for the Holy Spirit in some translations of the Gospel of John). The new priest surprised me with his answer. *It's a lovely quality that we have as human beings that God has blessed us on this Earth with free will – unlike the angels, for example, who know instantaneously what is right and wrong.* [39]

I may be wrong, Holy Father (and the new priest might be as well), but here is the full unabridged story of what Fr Emil believes to be happening in the Christian world today. For the limited time we have on Earth, there are two notional kingdoms: the kingdom of love and the kingdom of ego. The kingdom of love is dominated by God, who is perfect love; the kingdom of ego is dominated by Satan, who is the fallen angel and master of ego. Each of us has some level of ego which we need for our self-esteem, together with some level of love which we need for our relationships with others—including nature. God allows this struggle between love and ego as a fundamental aspect of free will, until the new outpouring of the Holy Spirit when we will lead lives with no ego, lives centered on the good of other people, including future generations. It's hard to imagine altruism on such a grand scale.

Fr Emil says we need God's grace to learn how to separate ourselves from our egos, to enable us to serve our communities. Our whole sense of being will be directed towards giving to others—that is when we will find our true freedom and discover who we really are. *What we will learn in the new era of the Holy Spirit is how to embark on the journey to complete freedom taken by the saints – how to surrender totally to God.*[40] So, there you have it—the irony of losing yourself to find true freedom. Anyone who loses their life for my sake will find it (Mt 16:26). No doubt the saints can surrender to God; but as for the rest of us, the prospects look daunting from where I stand.

Or from where I sat to be precise. Wardens at the grotto moved me along as other pilgrims waited to be seated in front of the makeshift altar, leaving me to stroll along the concrete and stone riverbank, wondering if something more could be done to help usher in the new era of the Holy Spirit—something more than I attempted to do at Medjugorje in the early 1990s. For a time, I put my shoulder to the wheel, until I grew weary of the uncertainty and loneliness of a spiritual life in the material world. Will anything be different this time around?

Sincerely
Peter Breen
Prodigal Pilgrim Group

Pilgrim Letter 5

An Underground Basilica for Contemplatives

Prodigal Pilgrim Group
Grand Hotel Moderne
21 Ave Bernadette Soubirous
Lourdes, France

July 22, 2019

Fr Jorge Mario Bergoglio
Holy Father Pope Francis
Papal Residence
Domus Sanctae Marthae
00120 Citta del Vaticano

Dear Fr Jorge

I spent my last day at Lourdes still wrestling with God—this time about physical healing—and exploring the shrine beyond the immediate precinct of the Massabielle grotto. But first, I drank from the spring that Bernadette unearthed, which today flows through pipes and spouts that line the walkway on either side of the grotto. Call it faith or superstition or childhood indoctrination, but one way or another, I reckon that Lourdes water can do wonders for any abnormal physical condition. Not the water itself, of course, but the grace that comes from the faith behind the supplications for healing—and not necessarily the faith of the sick person. In my childhood, most Catholic families had a bottle of Lourdes water, which was used to treat every conceivable ailment with faith, in the hope of a miraculous cure. As a child, I avoided the stuff, for fear of the greater affliction of putting God to the test, relying instead on my mother's faith in miracles.

These days, I get it. There are many explanations for physical healing besides divine intervention. I can believe in faith that God is responsible for a particularly striking cure, while recognizing that the laws of nature have not been broken. Even the most extraordinary cure that defies all the odds is not necessarily against nature or the natural order of things. There is such a thing as spontaneous remission, for example, and much of nature and the natural order is yet to be fully understood. A miracle is not something that happens contrary to nature; rather, it's contrary to *what is known of nature,* to quote St Augustine.[41] Miracles occur all the time in nature—water is turned into wine through the fermentation of grapes; loaves and fishes are multiplied with yeast and fish roe respectively; and inanimate food becomes new life in nature through assimilation.

Commenting on the devil's invitation to Jesus to turn stones into bread (Mt 4:3), CS Lewis observed that *the Son does nothing except what he sees the Father do: perhaps one may without boldness surmise that the direct change from stone to bread appeared to the Son to be not quite in the hereditary style. Little bread into much bread is quite a different matter.*[42] Some people who believe in the nature miracles draw the line at virgin birth according to Lewis, who was compelled to consider the question when he read a paper asserting that Christians believe in a God who had *committed adultery with the wife of a Jewish carpenter.*[43] Lewis' concern at the time of publication of the slur (1947) was that it reduced man to the role of sperm donor. But virgin birth is not contrary to nature in an era of invitro-fertilization—not to mention the abundance of hermaphroditism in nature.

The fantasy novel *The Erstwhile*, by author Brian Catling, is a story about the angels that failed to protect the Tree of Knowledge. A character named Schumann is described in the novel as *a rationalist who had spent his adult life wrestling with the testaments of divine intervention …* until his withered arm is cured by the angels. *Doubt in the form of healing had started to dissolve the rigid braces of opinion that he had insisted should hold all things in their sensible place.* It may be that natural forces were responsible for the healing. *But he knew what had happened. He knew it with a certainty that made all his sensible explanations candles to the sun. He knew that in some way those strange creatures had touched inside his brain and corrected the dam-*

aged tissue.[44] Schumann had no faith in physical healing—until it happened.

In an earlier letter, I mentioned that the Church has officially recognized as miracles only 70 of the thousands of cures at the Massabielle grotto, so I visited the Lourdes Medical Bureau for more information. Official cure number 70 was a French nun, Sr Bernadette Moriau, who was healed after being confined to a wheelchair with multiple disabilities for nearly 30 years. She attended a blessing for the sick at the Lourdes healing shrine in 2008, during celebrations to mark the 150th anniversary of Bernadette Soubirous' apparitions. On returning home three days later to her Franciscan community, she felt a surge of well-being and warmth while praying in the chapel. The next day she walked five kilometers with her sister. Importantly, Bernadette Moriau did not expect to be healed, and famously said she did not even ask for a miracle healing. You met this holy woman in the Vatican earlier this year, following the launch of her book about her unexpected cure.

I met another person who experienced a healing without expecting to receive one—in fact, he was bitterly opposed to the idea. That person was the Irish singer and professional footballer, David Parkes, who happened to be in Medjugorje a few years ago while I was there. Standing in the St James Church just a few rows ahead of me, a grey-headed man in a wind jacket suddenly burst into song, delivering the most exquisite version of 'Ave Maria' I had ever heard. Afterwards I shook his hand, thanking him for the musical treat, without having the foggiest clue who he was.

At age 27 at the peak of his two careers—singing and football—David Parkes was diagnosed with Crohn's disease. Over the next decade, he had ten major operations which ultimately proved to be futile, the last one in early 1989. His doctors gave him three months at most to live. His band held a benefit concert, to cover what were expected to be his funeral expenses. A man who attended the concert offered David and his wife, Ann, a free trip to Medjugorje which they knew about, as they had spent their honeymoon in nearby Dubrovnik.

David Parkes and God had parted company long ago. Religion had been banned in his house because David wanted nothing to do with a cruel God. He accepted the trip to Medjugorje as an opportunity to holiday again in Dubrovnik with his wife before he died. There were just two conditions: Ann was not to mention religion, nor to pray in his company. On the bus from Dubrovnik to Medjugorje, he went berserk when people started praying the rosary—he was almost put off the bus. The bus trip was excruciating enough due to his physical condition, without the added annoyance of people praying. When he reached the house of his host family in Medjugorje and found he did not have his own bathroom, he went berserk again, insisting that he must have his own facilities due to the difficulties of Crohn's disease. Ann promised to take him back to Dubrovnik the next day.

Before leaving Medjugorje—and against his better judgment—David agreed to attend a healing service with Fr Peter Rookey, a famous healing priest from the Servants of Mary religious order in Chicago. The priest placed a crucifix in David's hand and anointed him with oil, and then prayed with his hands resting on David's head. David went down like a sack of Irish potatoes. He felt an intense burning heat from the top of his head, traveling down through his body. From that day, all the symptoms of Crohn's disease disappeared and David was able to walk upright without pain. Back in Dublin, his surgeons conducted extensive tests *which confirmed there was no sign of Crohn's anywhere in David's body.*[45] David now works in Dublin as a pilgrimage director and gives regular free concerts in Medjugorje.

The point of these healing stories, Holy Father, is to illustrate something you already know—faith in God that brings about physical healing may be the faith of a friend or relative, or some other prayerful intercessor. When Jesus was asked by the centurion to cure his paralyzed servant he did so, saying let this be done for you [the centurion], as your faith demands (Mt 8:13). In another case, four men lowered a paralyzed man on a stretcher through the roof of a house, to get access to Jesus. Seeing their faith [the men on the roof], Jesus healed the paralytic (Mk 2:5). In some cases, the person healed may not even be aware of prayer intercessions (Bernadette Moriau) or may be actively opposed to the idea of healing grace (David Parkes). Even so, the great majority of people who are healed receive the grace through their own supplications. Jesus said to the woman who touched his cloak and was healed, your faith has restored you to health (Mk 5:34); and to the Samaritan cured of a virulent skin disease, your faith has made you well (Lk 17:19).

Less straightforward is why some people are cured through intercessory or other prayer, while some are not. There was a time when the crutches of those who were healed at Lourdes hung gratefully from the roof of the Massabielle grotto, a jumbled stalagmite testimony to the healing power of prayer. And then it dawned on somebody in authority at the Lourdes sanctuary that the number of pilgrims who do not receive a physical healing in response to their prayers far outweighs the lucky few who do. The crutches were a reminder of God's favor to the few and seeming indifference towards the many. Like any good democracy, the majority rules, so the Lourdes crutches were eventually removed.

In case I risk losing you again, I hasten to add that a miraculous healing in my correspondence is not so different at a spiritual level from an unsuccessful prayer for healing. This is something I hope to explore in another letter: the idea that conversion, and even transformation, is possible with or without healing.

Before signing off from Lourdes, Holy Father, I wanted to mention the eucharistic procession which occurs each day at five in the afternoon—a ceremony for the sick, as popular these days as the candlelight procession later in the evening. It begins at an open-air altar on the opposite side of the river to the grotto, proceeds across the bridge over the river, then down the esplanade to the entrance to the underground basilica named after your predecessor, Pope St Pius X. On a busy day, the basilica can seat 25,000 pilgrims, although you would never know it from the modest entrance at the side of the esplanade. From the back of the procession, the long line of sick and able-bodied pilgrims disappearing underground looks like a colony of ants returning to its nest. Down below, the cavernous basilica has a central concrete beam in the roof, supported by lateral beams that reach to the floor around the building's perimeter, giving visitors the impression that they are inside the rib cage of a giant whale.

Between the concrete ribs of the basilica, life-sized canvas reliefs depict the modern saints in no particular order, except perhaps the young Fatima visionaries, Francisco and Jacinta Marto, whose photographic images hang appositely alongside a painting of a gaunt-looking Polish priest, Fr Maximilian Kolbe. In the Auschwitz death camp, Kolbe gave his life in place of Franciszek Gajowniczek—one of ten random prisoners condemned to die of starvation in a small cell, as punishment for another prisoner who had escaped.

Gajowniczek survived Auschwitz and was present in Rome at Kolbe's canonization in 1971. Kolbe established his religious order dedicated to Marian devotion within days of Mary's last apparitions at Fatima in October 1917 (he was a young seminary student in Rome at the time) and spent much of his adult life writing about the extraordinary relationship between Mary and the Holy Spirit. Your predecessor, Pope John Paul II, visited Kolbe's death cell at Auschwitz in June 1979, and famously described the saintly priest as *the apostle of a new Marian era.*[46]

Perhaps better than anyone, Maximilian Kolbe wrote about the depth and intimacy of the unfathomable relationship between Mary and the Holy Spirit. More than just the 'spouse' of the Holy Spirit, Mary was *so to speak the personification of the Holy Spirit.*[47] Fr Kolbe explained further that Mary Immaculate is, in a certain sense, the 'incarnation' of the Holy Spirit. His writing assisted Vatican Council II in formulating the position of Mary in the Church as the *Mother of the Son of God... the beloved daughter of the Father and the temple of the Holy Spirit.*[48] The realization dawned on me at Lourdes that God is inextricably bound to our humanity through Mary according to Church teaching.

Fr Kolbe described Mary as God's most perfect creature. *For this reason, the homage paid to her is ... paid to God himself ... Why do we love Mary Immaculate and consecrate ourselves to her unreservedly? Not because of what she is in herself ... We love her because we love God.*[49] I paid homage myself to the saintly priest and holocaust victim before leaving the underground basilica and emerging into the twilight of my last night in Lourdes. In the distance, the upper basilica—the Basilica of the Immaculate Conception—was coming to life for the evening candlelight procession in a way I hadn't noticed before, its wide ramparts seeming to embrace the pilgrims and their flickering candles with outstretched welcoming arms.

Sincerely

Peter Breen

Prodigal Pilgrim Group

Part Two

The Secrets of Fatima 1917

Pilgrim Letter 6
Attending the Third Secret Obsequies

Prodigal Pilgrim Group
Hotel Santa Maria
Rota de Santo Antonio 79
Fatima, Portugal

August 5, 2019

Fr Jorge Mario Bergoglio
Holy Father Pope Francis
Papal Residence
Domus Sanctae Marthae
00120 Citta del Vaticano

Dear Fr Jorge

I arrived at Fatima in the hills of central Portugal by bus from Lisbon airport and checked into the Hotel Santa Maria, a swish establishment by the standards of my usual pilgrimage travel accommodation. Waiting for me in reception was the elegant and sophisticated Maria Joao Rodrigues de Araujo whose amazing network of friends and acquaintances includes a former minor party Australian politician. Maria lives just north of Fatima but spends much of her time in the United Kingdom, where she holds a doctorate in music from the University of Oxford and is a Fellow Commoner in Music at The Queen's College. These days, Maria's organizing commemorative celebrations for the London Treaty—the oldest diplomatic alliance still in force—between Portugal and England, a treaty signed at St Paul's Cathedral in London nearly 650 years ago.

It also happens that Maria is friends with Sr Angela Coelho, a religious sister and medical doctor based in Fatima, who is the vice-postulator for the cause for the canonization of Sr Lucia dos Santos—the principal visionary of Fatima. Sr Lucia died aged 97 years in 2005, after a lifetime of prayer and devotion as a teaching nun in Spain and discalced Carmelite nun in Portugal. I hope to meet Sr Angela who was also postulator for the cause of canonization of Lucia's younger cousins, Jacinta and Francisco Marto, who were present with Lucia during the Fatima apparitions of 1917. Forgive me for telling you things you must already know given that you canonized Jacinta and Francisco as saints on May 13, 2017 during the centenary celebrations of the first apparition at Fatima. I just wanted to put things into context. The bad news is that Sr Angela was out of town, and my friend Maria had less than an hour to spare before returning home. Over coffee, we looked at my draft submission to Sr Lucia's canonization inquiry, and Maria promised to pass on the final version to Sr Angela. In my respectful submission, Fatima's third secret should have died and gone to heaven in the year 2000, when Pope John Paul II released the full text of the prophecy.

You will recall, Holy Father, that Lucia was ten years old in 1917 when she was tending sheep with Jacinta and Francisco in the Cova da Iria on the outskirts of Fatima. In the early afternoon of May 13, under a clear blue sky, the children saw what they described as two flashes of lightning, followed by the appearance of what looked like *a Lady dressed all in white, more brilliant than the sun ... who was floating over a small holm oak shrub.*[50] Here is the conversation the children said took place between Lucia and 'the Lady' (described as 'Our Lady' and 'Your Grace' in the translation from Portuguese to English):

Our Lady: Do not be afraid; I will not harm you.

Lucia: Where is Your Grace from?

Our Lady: I am from heaven (Our Lady raised her hand and pointed to the sky).

Lucia: And what does Your Grace wish of me?

Our Lady: I have come to ask you to come here for six months in succession on the thirteenth day of each month at the same hour. Later I will tell you who I am and what I want [and then] I will return here a seventh time.

Lucia: And will I go to heaven too?

Our Lady: Yes, you will.

Lucia: And Jacinta?

Our Lady: Also.

Lucia: And Francisco?

Our Lady: Also, but he must say many Rosaries.

Lucia: Is Maria das Neves [a young woman who had died recently aged 16 years] already in heaven?

Our Lady: Yes, she is.

Lucia: And Amelia [another young woman who had died recently aged 18 to 20 years]?

Our Lady: She will be in purgatory until the end of the world.[51]

This last line of the conversation caused me alarm, Holy Father, bringing out both my inner defense lawyer and my outer sinful anger. In the criminal law, there is a principle called 'proportionality' in sentencing—the punishment should match the crime—and I wondered what heinous crime a young woman might commit to deserve such a harsh punishment. Alarm bells rang even louder when I learned that the young woman was complicit in some kind of 'immoral behavior'. What hope is there for any of us if 'immoral behavior' of any kind is deserving of such a punishment? Surely someone so young would be entitled to plead diminished responsibility, not to mention the age-old problem with hell and purgatory of unlimited punishment for limited human beings—otherwise known as cruel and unusual punishment in human rights law. The fate of the young woman (whose name I always associate with 'ameliorate') always bothers me. I do not understand how a just and merciful God can take immorality—in any of its many manifestations—so seriously. Perhaps I can seek your guidance in a separate letter, Holy Father, given that you have written quite extensively on the God of mercy and the problem of evil. Anyway, I apologize for wandering off country, and I will return to Lucia's conversation with the Lady.

Lucia reported that the Lady *opened her hands, which emitted an intense light [and then she asked the children to] pray the Rosary every day to obtain peace for the world and the end of the war [World War I] ... Then the Lady began to rise serenely toward the east until she disappeared far into the distance.* [52] Following the first apparition, Lucia was scolded for telling lies, and sent to the parish priest to confess her sins. About 50 spectators turned up at the Cova da Iria for the second apparition on June 13, 1917. *Precisely at noon the Lady in light appeared above the holm oak again, and though she was invisible to the onlookers, everyone saw what seemed to be a small white cloud of light float down from the eastern sky and hover over the little tree where the children were kneeling in ecstasy.* [53] Again, the Lady opened her hands to emit light, which coincided with the sun becoming noticeably dimmer. [54]

The next day, Lucia was again chastised by her mother, Maria Rosa, for lying about the apparitions, and taken to the parish priest's house for further interrogation. Before entering the house, Maria Rosa upbraided her youngest child. *Tell the Reverend Father now that you lied, so that on Sunday he can say in the church that it was all a lie, and that will be the end of the whole affair. A nice business this is! All this crowd running to the Cova da Iria, just to pray in front of a holm oak bush!*[55]

Lucia's mother was the least of the child's troubles after the third apparition on July 13, 1917 when she received three secrets.

The first secret was a vision of hell:

Lucia:

Our Lady opened Her hands once more, as She had done during the two previous months. The rays of light seemed to penetrate the earth, and we saw as it were a sea of fire. Plunged in this fire were demons and souls in human form, like transparent burning embers, all blackened or burnished bronze, floating about in the conflagration, now raised into the air by the flames that issued from within themselves together with great clouds of smoke ... This vision lasted but an instant. How can we ever be grateful enough to our kind heavenly Mother, who had already prepared us by promising, in the first Apparition, to take us to Heaven. Otherwise, I think we would have died of fear and terror.[56]

The second secret was the Lady's prophecy:

Our Lady:

> *You have seen hell where the souls of poor sinners go. To save them, God wishes to establish in the world devotion to my Immaculate Heart. If what I say is done, many souls will be saved and there will be peace. The war [World War I] is going to end, but if people do not cease offending God, a worse one [World War II] will break out during the pontificate of Pius XI. When you see a night illumined by an unknown light, know that this is the great sign given you by God that He is about to punish the world for its crimes, by means of war, famine, and persecutions of the Church and of the Holy Father. To prevent this, I shall come to ask for the consecration of Russia to my Immaculate Heart, and the Communion of reparation on the First Saturdays. If my requests are heeded, Russia will be converted, and there will be peace; if not, she will spread her errors throughout the world causing wars and persecutions of the Church. The good will be martyred; the Holy Father will have much to suffer; and various nations will be annihilated. In the end, my Immaculate Heart will triumph. The Holy Father will consecrate Russia to*

me, and she will be converted, and a period of peace will be granted to the world.[57]

The third secret was a symbolic revelation:

Lucia:

> *After the two parts [the three secrets are sometimes described as one secret in three parts] which I have already explained, at the left of Our Lady and a little above, we saw an Angel with a flaming sword in his left hand; flashing, it gave out flames that looked as though they would set the world on fire, but they died out in contact with the splendor that Our Lady radiated towards him from her right hand. Pointing to the earth with his right hand, the Angel cried out in a loud voice: Penance, Penance, Penance. And we saw in an immense light that is God ... a Bishop dressed in White (we had the impression it was the Holy Father). Other Bishops, Priests, men and women Religious [were] going up a steep mountain, at the top of which there was a big Cross ... [at] the top of the mountain, on his knees at the foot of the big Cross he [the Bishop dressed in White] was killed by a group of soldiers who fired bullets and arrows at him, and*

in the same way there died one after another the oth-
er Bishops, men and women Religious. [58]

You may not be aware of the full controversy surrounding the third secret, Holy Father, so here it is in a nutshell.
Unlike the first and second secrets, Mary's voice was missing in the third secret—she made no comment on the reported vision as she did the vision of hell. Frightening as it
was, the language of the first two secrets depicted real places or states and real events, while the words of the third secret are allegorical and open to many possible interpreta-
tions. Another popular objection to the third secret is that it
was written on one sheet of paper, whereas the copy released by the Vatican was a photocopy in four pages. The
last popular objection is that the third secret comprises two
parts, not one, and the two parts are contained in two separate envelopes. Objectors insist that while the allegorical
part of the third secret in the first envelope was released in
the year 2000, the remaining explanatory part in the second
envelope has never been made public.

The best book on Fatima in my opinion is *Fatima for*
Today: The Urgent Marian Message of Hope written by the
late Fr Andrew Apostoli, who says that the emphasis on
penance in the third secret is a reference to the need for
conversion or a change of heart, *a real turning away from*
sin and toward God. [59] In an appendix to the book, Apostoli
deals with each of the popular objections to the third secret,

making the point that everyone who read it under three popes confirmed that the full text of the secret was released by your predecessor, Pope John Paul II. At the same time, the then prefect of the Congregation for the Doctrine of the Faith, Joseph Cardinal Ratzinger, issued a commentary on the third secret, in which he affirmed that the events predicted had already occurred. *Insofar as individual events are described, they belong to the past. Those who expected exciting apocalyptic revelations about the end of the world or the future course of history [will] be disappointed.*[60]

Sr Lucia and Pope John Paul II both said that the 'Bishop in White' who was 'killed' in the allegorical third secret was a reference to Mehmet Ali Agca's attempt to shoot the pope at close range in St Peter's Square in Vatican City on May 13, 1981. The great pope had a deep devotion to Mary and believed she directed the two bullets that entered his body that day—one bullet in the abdomen should have killed him but for the trajectory it followed, narrowly missing vital organs. His affection for Fatima is everywhere to be seen at the sanctuary, from his bronze statue at the entrance to the modernist-design Basilica of the Holy Trinity to the Museum of the Shrine of Fatima, where he has more secondary relics on display—including the bullet that nearly killed him—than any other saint on the liturgical calendar.

The first two secrets were revealed in Sr Lucia's 1941 memoirs, while the third secret was written down around

January 9, 1944, when the nun informed Bishop Jose da Silva of Leiria that she had complied with his request to commit the secret to writing. Seven days earlier, Sr Lucia had been in a state of turmoil about whether to release the third secret. *Our Lady appeared to the nun on January 2, 1944 and told her to write the third part of the Secret. This apparition happened because the seer did not know what to do, as the Bishop of Leiria had ordered her to write it and the Archbishop of Valladolid, who took over the diocese of Tuy, told her not to.*[61] Controversy still surrounds the way Sr Lucia wrote down the third secret and whether she placed it in one envelope or two. Apostoli appears to be aware of this controversy in *Fatima for Today,* suggesting that the envelope containing the third secret was placed inside a slightly larger outer envelope. Sr Lucia read and checked the document just a couple of weeks before it was due to be made public on May 13, 2000, and informed Archbishop Tarcisio Bertone, the then secretary for the Congregation for the Doctrine of the Faith: *Yes, this is the Third Secret, and I never wrote any other.*[62]

With the benefit of Sr Lucia's testimony, and the testimony of your immediate predecessors Benedict XVI and John Paul II, the argument for getting off the case of the third secret is a strong one. Even so, objectors remain concerned about the two envelopes containing the third secret. Sr Lucia wrote on the outside of both envelopes: *By express order of Our Lady, this envelope can only be opened in 1960*

by the cardinal Patriarch of Lisbon or the Bishop of Leiria.
Tarcisio Bertone (by then elevated to Cardinal) presented
both envelopes on Italian national television on May 31,
2007. A year later, the cardinal published a book in which
he insisted there was only one envelope.[63] An inference can
be drawn that two envelopes containing separate texts exist
and the content of the second envelope—Mary's explanation for the meaning of the vision—is yet to be released by
the Vatican. Other evidence supports the inference, including Vatican press releases in 1960 and statements attributed
to Loris Capovilla, who was secretary to Pope John XXIII.

You will not be surprised to learn that I examined the
issues around the third secret in a book of fiction that
turned out to be a hat full of bother. My story of the missing second envelope, with its explosive revelations about
the future, was a plot worthy of a Dan Brown novel. Fortu-
nately, nobody wanted to publish the book, which one New
York publisher described as having poorly constructed dialogue, wooden characters, and an unbelievable plot.

These days, I have no illusion that the third secret of
Fatima has anything more to tell us beyond what was revealed by your two predecessors in the year 2000. I would
like to conclude by saying that Fatima's second secret is
much more interesting than the third since the triumph of
Mary's heart and the promised period of peace are prophecies yet to be fulfilled. And you will forgive me for reminding you that the Church approved Fatima 'worthy of belief

as private revelation' even while the prophecies remained outstanding—a precedent worth noting as you duly consider the Medjugorje apparitions.

Sincerely

Peter Breen

Prodigal Pilgrim Group

Pilgrim Letter 7
The Unfulfilled Second Secret Prophecy

Prodigal Pilgrim Group
Hotel Santa Maria
Rota de Santo Antonio 79
Fatima, Portugal

August 10, 2019

Fr Jorge Mario Bergoglio
Holy Father Pope Francis
Papal Residence
Domus Sanctae Marthae
00120 Citta del Vaticano

Dear Fr Jorge

As I walked in the Vatican Gardens on November 18, 1990, admiring the greenery, I was greatly surprised when the double gates to my left opened unexpectedly, and a large Russian limousine crunched its way along the gravel driveway towards the official tradesman's entrance to the Apostolic Palace. As the vehicle passed by, the Soviet Union's president, Mikhail Gorbachev, gave me a wave from the open window in the nearside front passenger seat. It was his second visit to your predecessor, Pope John Paul II, in less than a year. A year later, Gorbachev would resign as president on the morning of December 25, 1991, and the Soviet Union would cease to exist. Later that same day, the Soviet hammer and sickle flag was lowered over the Kremlin for the last time, to be replaced by the Russian Federation's red, white and blue tricolor flag. *People all over the world watched in amazement at this relatively peaceful transition from former Communist monolith into multiple separate nations.*[64]

Was this the conversion of Russia promised by 'the Lady' who appeared in apparition at Fatima in 1917? Before addressing that question, Holy Father, I should tell you how I happened to be in the Vatican Gardens on that day in 1990.

I arrived in Rome to research my book about Fatima's third secret, armed with a letter of introduction to Marjorie Weekes of the Pontifical Council for Social Communications from the eminent Australian writer, Morris West, who had just completed a documentary film of life in the Vatican. West was one of Dr Weekes' heroes, so the letter worked a treat—the woman in charge of the Vatican communications office put a press identity card in the top pocket of my jacket and placed a camera on a long strap over my shoulder. *Follow me* she said, and off we went at a quickening pace through a rabbit warren of corridors and walkways, finally emerging into a room that looked like a bambino auditorium, where Pope John Paul II was receiving a delegation of bishops and priests from Africa. I joined half a dozen journalists with real press credentials on a raised platform to the side of the room—about ten yards from the pope.

As the last of the Africans was leaving, the pope wandered over and blessed the journalists and their ring-in. He chatted briefly to one journalist before being whisked away by a couple of clerics. The journalists dispersed and I followed Dr Weekes back to her office, where she organized a researcher's pass that gave me access to the Archivio Segreto Vaticano (the 'Vatican Secret Archives') at the back of the Vatican Museums. I was pretty much speechless with gratitude. As you know, each new pope is the official custodian of the archives, which include more than 50 miles of shelf space housing documents, correspondence, books, scrolls, and parchments dating back to the first century of Christianity. Dr Weekes asked about my book and suggested I travel on pilgrimage to Medjugorje before writing another word about Fatima. I had never heard of Medjugorje but promised to check it out.

Leaving the communications office, I wandered through the Vatican Gardens in a bit of daze, and that was when the back gates opened and the limousine carrying the Russian president rolled in. So, with a blessing from the saintly John Paul II and a wave from the enigmatic Gorbachev, I may have been on hand for the conversion of Russia.

Just a couple of days earlier, I had travelled to Rome after a life-changing experience at Fatima, where I had returned to the faith after an absence of more than 20 years. It's difficult to recall now what happened in 1990, but I remember standing in front of the Basilica of Our Lady of the Rosary in the Fatima sanctuary, trying to recall the joyful, sorrowful, and glorious mysteries of the rosary—a prayer I had not recited since I was a teenager in the seminary. Today, I still get goosebumps at Fatima, and the light is always amazing somehow, as though still electrified by those flashes of lightning that came out of the blue at the Cova in 1917.

Mary appeared at Fatima between Russia's two revolutions of 1917 —the February Revolution in which Czar Nicholas II abdicated and the October Revolution in which the Bolshevik Party, led by Vladimir Lenin, took control in a coup against the Russian parliament's provisional government. Following the October revolution, Lenin became the world's first Communist dictator, leading the Red Army in a devastating civil war that killed more than eight million Russian soldiers and civilians. Lenin accused the opposing White Army of prosecuting the civil war *to restore the dictatorship of the bourgeoisie, the power of the landowners, and the monarchy.*[65]

In her July 1917 appearance at Fatima, Mary prophesied that *the Holy Father will consecrate Russia to me, and she will be converted.*[66] It's generally agreed that this consecration of Russia did not take place as instructed, until your predecessor, Pope John Paul II, visited the Fatima shrine and made the consecration on March 25, 1984. This has given rise to further objections that the conversion of Russia is another unfulfilled prophecy of Fatima. Objectors say that the collapse of Russian Communism could be regarded as a conversion, but not the conversion contemplated by the rest of the Fatima story—a change of heart and turning away from sin. The argument runs that Russia has merely switched from one form of dictatorship to another.

What can be said with confidence is that, under Gorbachev, Russia notionally made the epic journey from totalitarian state to democratic republic, and in that sense, Russia was converted. The confused ideas of atheistic humanism—humanity 'liberated' from God—came down with the final lowering of the hammer and sickle flag over the Kremlin on Christmas Day in 1991. Gorbachev was ultimately disappointed by the effectiveness of 'glasnost' (openness) and 'perestroika' (restructuring), due to what he saw as the failure of Western countries to support his initiatives. He talked with President George Bush Senior and Pope John Paul II about creating a new world order that would be more just, humane, and secure than its predecessor, but it never happened. The Americans were intent upon creating a new empire headed by themselves,[67] while the Vatican seemed to be oversensitive to the new legitimacy achieved by the Russian Orthodox Church in the Gorbachev era.

Pope John Paul II refused to go on pilgrimage to Russia, in the absence of an invitation from its orthodox church leaders.[68]

Pope John Paul II often spoke about 'a new springtime' in the Church which he saw as the fruit of the Second Vatican Ecumenical Council, a momentous gathering of the faithful described by the saintly pope as the greatest spiritual experience in the Roman Catholic Church since Pentecost. He did not live to see the new springtime. *But we can believe that Pope John Paul II knew the new springtime would eventually come, as would Our Lady of Fatima's promise that in the end Russia would be converted and her Immaculate Heart would triumph.*[69] In this quote, Fr Apostoli seems to be saying that Russia is still not converted, but I am inclined to draw a line under the prophecies at Fatima, Holy Father, and to suggest they are fulfilled—except for Mary's triumph and peace in the world. Russia is converted in the context of the prophecies according to both your predecessors, Pope Benedict XVI and Pope John Paul II.

One other aspect of the July 13, 1917 revelations needs to be addressed, and it relates to the credibility of the apparitions, given the tender ages of the child visionaries. Jacinta and Francisco Marto were aged just seven and nine years respectively at the beginning of the apparitions in 1917. Both were victims of the 1918 Spanish flu pandemic, dying aged ten and eleven years, respectively. Although Lucia dos

Santos lived to the age of 97 years, she was aged just 12 years at the time of the apparitions.

The Church relied almost exclusively on Lucia's testimony for the content of Mary's messages. Supporters of the apparitions point out that Jesus—filled with joy by the Holy Spirit—thanked the Father for hiding these things from the learned and the clever and revealing them to little children (Lk 10:21). Most people I know agree that the youth of the visionaries—at both Lourdes and Fatima—enhanced their credibility, especially when information came out of their mouths with no conceivable origin other than the apparitions.

Even so, some delicate matters arise by virtue of the ages of the children at Fatima. Jacinta, the youngest of the three child visionaries, was told by 'the Lady' that the sins that lead most souls to hell are sins of the flesh. The child had no idea what this meant so spoke to her mother about it. I was reminded of poor Amelia, a child sentenced to purgatory until the end of the world for immoral behavior. Already she has served 103 years in earthly terms.

Another difficulty arising out of the tender ages of the children on July 13, 1917, came to light in Lucia's report of the conversation with the Lady on that day. Lucia agreed on behalf of the three children, to offer their earthly sufferings in reparation for sin and the conversion of sinners, an agreement no earthly court would be likely to recognize and one that the children would scarcely be able to comprehend.

> *Our Lady: Do you wish to offer yourselves to God to endure all the sufferings that He may be pleased to send you, as both an act of reparation for the sins with which he is offended and supplication for the conversion of sinners?*
>
> *Lucia: Yes, we do.*
>
> *Our Lady: Well then, you will have much to suffer. But the grace of God will be your comfort.*[70]

Children are no more likely to understand the nature of this commitment than they would be capable of comprehending sins of the flesh. What may be missing, of course, is my capacity to understand God's way of doing things. Despite the difficulties, Fatima's simple message of conversion and penance to avoid destruction and chaos in the world should be taken seriously in my correspondence, primarily because of the innocence of the messengers. The message is the same as that given to Bernadette Soubirous at Lourdes—pray for sinners and do penance for conversion. And then there is the fact that Fatima has received unqualified support from a long line of popes since Vatican Council II beginning with Pope John XXIII who described the Fatima message as *the world's greatest hope for peace.*[71] For the golden jubilee of the apparitions on May 13, 1967,

Pope Paul VI *journeyed to Fatima 'as a humble pilgrim' to 'pray for peace' in the presence of a million pilgrims from all over the world.*[72]

A million pilgrims turned up again at Fatima on May 13, 2017 to commemorate 100 years since the first apparition at the Cova da Iria and to celebrate the canonization of Francisco and Jacinta Marto. You greeted pilgrims in the Chapel of the Apparitions, reminding them that God's judgment will always be rendered in the light of his mercy. *Great injustice is done to God's grace whenever we say that sins are punished by his judgement, without first saying—as the Gospel clearly does—that they are forgiven by his mercy.*[73] Your words of consolation were powerful, reminding me of the need to always remain open to the possibility of further enlightenment and greater holiness, to better understand the way God's grace works.

I have more to report concerning the apparitions at Fatima in August, September, and October of 1917, leading up to the solar miracle which was witnessed by perhaps 100,000 people within a 30-mile radius of the village. For the benefit of order and convenience, I will conclude this letter, Holy Father, and then return to each of the three remaining Fatima apparitions in separate letters.

Sincerely
Peter Breen
Prodigal Pilgrim Group

Pilgrim Letter 8

Cause for Concern at the August Apparition

Prodigal Pilgrim Group

Hotel Santa Maria

Rota de Santo Antonio 79

Fatima, Portugal

August 15, 2019

Fr Jorge Mario Bergoglio

Holy Father Pope Francis

Papal Residence

Domus Sanctae Marthae

00120 Citta del Vaticano

Dear Fr Jorge

A crowd of some 15,000 locals and visitors gathered around the small holm oak shrub at the Cova da Iria on August 13,1917, expecting to witness the fourth visitation of 'the Lady' to the child Lucia dos Santos and her younger cousins Francisco and Jacinta Marto. News that the children had been given a secret and were promised a public miracle in October had swelled the numbers trampling down the vegetables and sheep pastures planted by Lucia's father in his small landholding. What the anxious crowd did not know was that the young visionaries had been kidnapped by a local public official, Arturo Santos, the local magistrate, and civic administrator of the district of Fatima.

As the midday appointment with the miraculous visitor approached, with still no sign of the children, a whisper of their fate began buzzing around the crowd. A young woman, Maria de Carreira, who had stood with the children during the two previous apparitions (and would later become the first custodian of the Fatima shrine) reported that the absence of the children made the crowd grow restless, until a large clap of thunder and blinding flash of light diverted everyone's attention.

When it became known that the magistrate had kidnapped [the children], a terrible resentment went through the crowd. There is no telling what it might have turned into, had it not thundered just then. Some thought the thunder came from the road; others thought it came from the holm oak; but it seemed to me that it came from a distance. It frightened us all and many began to cry, fearing they were going to be killed. Of course, no one was killed … Right after the thunder came the flash [the opposite of a natural phenomenon], and immediately, we all noticed a little cloud, very white, beautiful and bright, that came and stayed over the holm oak. It remained a few minutes, then rose towards the heavens where it disappeared. Looking about, we noticed a strange sight that we had already seen and would see again. Everyone's faces glowed rose, red, blue—all the colors of the rainbow. The trees seemed to have no branches or leaves but were all covered with flowers; every leaf was a flower. The ground was in little squares, each one a different color. Our clothes seemed to be transformed into the colors of the rainbow.[74]

Early in the afternoon following the dramatic events at the Cova da Iria, many in the crowd confronted the local parish priest, Fr Manuel Ferreira, who they suspected was complicit in kidnapping the children. Protesting his innocence, the priest apologized for not attending that day during the promised apparition. *If my absence from the Cova gave offence to believers, my presence would have been no less objectionable to unbelievers. The Blessed Virgin has no need of the parish priest in order to manifest her goodness.*[75]

Two days later, on August 15, the priest was on hand when the children were returned to the rectory by car, the driver almost causing a riot when his arrival coincided with the congregation emerging from the adjoining church, after attending Mass to celebrate the feast of the Assumption of Mary into Heaven. Some people still blamed the priest for the children's abduction and it fell to Ti Marto, the father of Francisco and Jacinta, to intervene and say that God had allowed this ordeal to happen and the children were un-harmed.

Lucia wrote in her memoirs that she was deeply hurt on returning home from her imprisonment to find that her parents showed no sign of welcome or even relief that she had come to no harm. *What I felt most deeply and what caused me most suffering on that occasion was my being completely abandoned by my family ... To celebrate my arrival [home], they sent me right away to let out the sheep and take them off to pasture.*[76] On Sunday, August 19, the young visionary accompanied the sheep to a place called Valinhos, about a mile from Fatima, where she was soon joined by Francisco and his older brother John.

Later in the day, Lucia sensed that 'the Lady' was about to appear and sent John to fetch Jacinta. The brightness of the sun faded, the air grew cooler, and Lucia and Francisco saw the flash of light. At Jacinta's arrival, there was a second flash and the three children saw the Lady in light standing on a nearby tree, although John saw nothing. The Lady en-couraged the children to pray the rosary every day, to con-tinue going to the Cova on the thirteenth of the month, and she repeated the promise to perform a public miracle in October—although the miracle would be reduced, due to the way the civil authorities had treated the children.

I wondered about God understating the power of a pub-lic miracle that you and I might have wanted to enhance—if only to slap down the conniving magistrate—although it may be presumptuous of me to anticipate your reaction. One author explained that the proposed miracle of the sun was diminished in the same way that sin diminishes God's grace for everyone. Think Adam and Eve and the disproportionate consequences for humanity of their sin. Another author compared sin (opposition to God's plan) as having a similar effect to a lack of faith diminishing God's miraculous power.[77] Jesus had difficulty performing miracles in his hometown of Nazareth, where people had little faith in the local carpenter's son. These are difficult matters, Holy Father, and I would value your perspective on them.

You may also be interested in Lucia's plea, during this apparition, for 'the Lady' to heal some sick people, to which she replied: *'Yes, I will cure some of them during the year.' Then, looking very sad, ['the Lady'] said: 'Pray ... and make sacrifices for sinners; for many souls go to hell, because there are none to sacrifice themselves and to pray for them'.*[78]

A profound truth about hell is hidden in plain sight in these words—the living can save sinners who otherwise seem to have no capacity to save themselves. It seems to be the case that God allows souls otherwise destined for hell to slip quietly into purgatory in response to our prayers and sacrifices. Once again as a lawyer, I struggle with the principle of proportionality in sentencing, and the seeming imbalance between modest prayers and sacrifices as a trade-off for eternal punishment.

In her book, *My Heart Will Triumph*, Mirjana Soldo said she found the concept of hell difficult to understand even after the apparitions at Medjugorje began. In human terms, a prisoner serves his sentence and is forgiven his crime, while sentencing a soul to an eternity of suffering seemed contrary to the merciful and loving God. One day, during a Marian apparition, Mirjana asked how God could be so unmerciful as to condemn people to hell for eternity. *'Souls who go to Hell have ceased thinking favorably of God,' Our Lady told me. In life they cursed Him, she explained, and in death they will continue to do the same. In essence, they've already become part of Hell. God does not send people to Hell. They choose to be there.*[79]

The idea that the damned exercise their free will to deliberately choose the place or state we call hell is one that seems to be at odds with human experience, Holy Father. I have known several prisoners sentenced to life in prison. Almost without exception, they would prefer a death sentence to draw a line under their punishment. Given a choice, prisoners spend every waking hour thinking about how to get released from their suffering, not about perpetuating their miserable existence. Eternal punishment is synonymous with cruel and inhumane treatment by the standards of secular justice, with no opportunity for reprieve. My human perception of justice—the proportionality principle in sentencing —is turned on its head by the notion that the damned have no desire for any other form of existence beyond eternal punishment. It goes without saying, that I defer to the revelation that the damned do in fact choose their own fate, even though I fail to comprehend the choice.

At the conclusion of the August 19 apparition at Fatima, the children's vision of 'the Lady' along with the cloud of white light rose in the sky to the east and disappeared. The children noticed that the tree on which the apparition stood gave off a sweet fragrance, and they broke off some sprays, taking one back to Lucia's mother who remained incredulous about the apparitions until asked to smell the foliage. *The sudden awareness of the incredibly beautiful fragrance jolted Maria Rosa; for the first time she began to wonder if there was not some truth in the children's story after all.*[80]

Please excuse the brevity and lack of formality in the last couple of letters from Fatima, Holy Father, but I seem to be spending more time exploring the shrine, enjoying the company of my fellow pilgrims, and putting off the solitude of my writing desk in the hotel room.

Sincerely
Peter Breen
Prodigal Pilgrim Group

Pilgrim Letter 9

Confidence in the September Apparition

Prodigal Pilgrim Group

Hotel Santa Maria

Rota de Santo Antonio 79

Fatima, Portugal

August 21, 2019

Fr Jorge Mario Bergoglio

Holy Father Pope Francis

Papal Residence

Domus Sanctae Marthae

00120 Citta del Vaticano

Dear Fr Jorge

In their endeavors to suppress the claims of the three children, who insisted that a visitor from another world was appearing at Fatima's Cova da Iria, the public authorities succeeded only in creating speculation and interest in the affair. Undeterred by the official warning to stay away, thousands more pilgrims and spectators turned up on the morning of September 13, 1917 (the fifth apparition) than were present in August. Some hoped to bear witness to the extraordinary events, others wanted merely to confirm their suspicions of a fraud. Many witnesses gave evidence that as the scheduled time for the mysterious visitation drew near, *there was a sudden cooling of the air, and the sun was dimmed, so much so that thousands of people could see the stars even though it was midday. Also, there was a rain of iridescent petals that vanished upon reaching the ground.*[81]

The apparition is recorded in Lucia's memoirs:

As the hour approached, I set out with Jacinta and Francisco, but owing to the crowds around us we could only advance with difficulty. The roads were packed with people, and everyone wanted to see us and speak to us. There was no human respect whatsoever. Simple folk, and even ladies and gentlemen, struggled to break through the crowd that pressed around us. No sooner had they reached us than they threw themselves on their knees before us, begging us to place their petitions before Our Lady. Others who could not get close to us shouted from a distance: 'For the love of God, ask Our Lady to cure my son who is a cripple!' Yet another cried out: 'And to cure mine who is blind! ... To cure mine who is deaf! ... To bring back my husband, my son, who has gone to the war! ... To convert a sinner! ... To give me back my health as I have tuberculosis!' and so on... All the afflictions of poor humanity were assembled there. Some climbed up to the tops of trees and walls to see us go by and shouted down to us. Saying yes to some, giving a hand to others and helping them up from the dusty ground, we managed to move forward, thanks to some gentlemen who went ahead ... At last, we arrived at the Cova da Iria, and on reaching the holm oak we began to say the Rosary with the people. Shortly afterwards, we saw the flash of light, and then Our Lady appeared on the holm oak.

Our Lady: Continue to pray the Rosary in order to obtain the end of the war. In October Our Lord will come, as well as Our Lady of Sorrows and Our Lady of Mount Carmel. Saint Joseph will appear with the Child Jesus to bless the world. God is pleased with your sacrifices. He does not want you to sleep with the rope on, but only to wear it during the daytime [the children had taken to tying rope around their waists as an act of penance for the souls of sinners].

Lucia: I was told to ask you many things, the cure of some sick people, of a deaf mute...

Our Lady: Yes, I will cure some, but not others. In October I will perform a miracle so that all may believe.

Then Our Lady began to rise as usual and disappeared.[82]

One of the visitors to the Cova da Iria that day was the vicar general of Leiria, Monsignor John Quaresma, who reported what he witnessed. *At noontime, silence fell on the crowd, and a low whispering of prayers could be heard. Suddenly, cries of joy rent the air, many voices praising the Blessed Virgin. Arms were raised to point to something above ... There was not a single cloud in the whole blue sky, yet to my great astonishment, I saw clearly and distinctly a luminous globe, coming from the east to the west, gliding slowly and majestically through space.*[83] Afterwards, the monsignor and one of his priest colleagues conducted random discussions with the people around them to inquire what they had seen. *The persons interrogated were of the most various classes; yet with one voice they affirmed the reality of the phenomena which we had contemplated ... Deeply satisfied, we returned home from our pilgrimage to Fatima, with the firm purpose of coming back on the thirteenth of October to accede to Lucia's invitation and to fortify even more our faith in the apparitions.*

A curious aspect of the monsignor's testimony, Holy Father, was his recollection of a clear blue sky, while the simultaneous perception of others was a diminution of the sun's intensity at midday, to the point where stars were visible as in a night sky. Others present witnessed nothing unusual, according to the monsignor. *For on all sides were heard manifestations of joy, and greetings to Our Lady. Some, however, saw nothing; one good and pious soul nearby wept bitterly for not having seen.*[84]

At Medjugorje, I discovered that people see the same paranormal phenomenon differently—or perhaps not at all—and nothing turns on the different perceptions of God's grace. I was going to say that something similar happens when some people and not others are healed, but I may need the benefit of your insight on that proposition.

I noticed that older translations of the September 13 dialogue with 'the Lady' (who had still not disclosed her name) included additional material which is omitted from recent editions of Lucia's memoirs. After her request for a cure for some sick people including *of a deaf mute …* the following discussion took place.

> *Lucia: This girl is a deaf mute. Don't you want to cure her?*
>
> *Our Lady: In the course of the year, she will be improved.*
>
> *Lucia: Will you help these other people?*
>
> *Our Lady: Some I will cure; but the others, no. Our Lord does not have confidence in them.*

Callous as it may seem, the proposition I would like to advance is that God deliberately holds back physical healing in some cases where a higher benefit may accrue to a person from continued suffering. CS Lewis expressed the idea in *The Problem of Pain*, published during World War II. *God whispers to us in our pleasures, speaks in our conscience, but shouts in our pain: it is His megaphone to arouse a deaf world ... No doubt pain as God's megaphone is a terrible instrument; it may lead to final and unrepented rebellion. But it gives the only opportunity the bad man can have for amendment. It removes the veil; it plants the flag of truth within the fortress of a rebel soul.*[85] With the insight of a great Irish writer, Lewis knew the solution he offered to the problem of unmitigated pain would attract condemnation. *All arguments in justification of suffering provoke bitter resentment against the author ... I am only trying to show that the old Christian doctrine of being made 'perfect through suffering' is not incredible. To prove it palatable is beyond my design.*[86]

In his second letter to the Corinthians, the Apostle Paul said he asked the Lord to remove a thorn in the flesh (2 Cor 12:7). Then he decided to suffer the thorn—some disability or infirmity—for the good of the Christian cause when God told him that grace is enough, for power is at full stretch in weakness (2 Cor 12:9). In his letter to the Colossians, Paul seemed to be talking about redemptive suffering, when he wrote about offering his own suffering in union with Jesus' suffering on the cross (Col 1:24).

Another thing that concerns me about God's confidence being a prerequisite to healing is that like the Apostle Paul, we are all called in one way or another to be saints—even when we have been the worst of sinners. And it would not have escaped your attention that very few of the saints (none that comes to mind) has escaped earthly suffering. I asked Fr Emil Milat what he thought of unanswered prayers for healing, and he reminded me that anything we ask of the Father in Jesus' name we will receive through the gifts of the Holy Spirit, although not necessarily in a form we expect or comprehend. But the priest insisted that no prayers go unanswered—especially prayers for healing—even if the answer is delayed or its meaning remains obscure.

Fr Emil did offer some encouragement for those of us whose spiritual or physical healing continues to elude God's mercy: always keep praying for healing, always keep asking for mercy. *If God wants you to carry a sickness or burden in what is a reparatory suffering, you will receive a grace to see the good of what that suffering is doing.*[87] Avoid the heresy of Jansenism—life is hard, life is tough. Some of the saints suffered terribly, but they had a deep interior awareness that their suffering was transformative. God's love and mercy transform us even when we appear not to receive physical healing. *What's important is transformation, whether through healing or continued suffering.*[88]

If I think about my relationship with God in human terms, I can quite easily imagine how God might lack confidence in the relationship, based on my previous behavior in situations where I was not to be trusted. And yes, human love has its limitations—I cannot assume that God's love is unconditional like that of a doting parent who sees no fault in their child. It seems to me that a just and perfect God is inconsistent with unrequited love. Surely the great mystery is that any of us is healed. There may be gratuitous healing on God's part, Holy Father, along with disappointment for many with deep faith who remain chained to their litters and wheelchairs. I doubt that everyone who is healed inspires God's confidence—think about the ten lepers who were healed and only one returned to give thanks and praise to God (Lk 17:11-19). I would be interested to know where you think God draws a line in the sand against those of us who fall short in our supplications for the grace of healing.

I like to remember the importunate widow who complained incessantly for justice to the unsympathetic judge lacking compassion for her circumstances; until finally he relented, in order not to be driven mad by the woman's pleas for relief from her suffering (Lk 18:1-8). God is no unjust judge, of course, and has the benefit of omniscience to call on when assessing the potential for healing grace. What we do have at our disposal—those of us likely to lack the confidence of God—is the intercession of Mary to argue our case, just as she did at the wedding feast of Cana when they had no wine. Ignoring Jesus' objections, she told the servants to do whatever her son told them (Jn 2:4-5).

I should mention, Holy Father, that tomorrow is my last day in Fatima. It seems fitting to be leaving as I report on the events of the final day of the apparitions—the day of the Miracle of the Sun. I look forward to reviewing what happened at Fatima in the context of the prophecies at Medjugorje. You will not be too interested in speculation about the future, I know, but if the way we live is unsustainable, and we are unable or unwilling to do something about that because we believe we lack the power to change the status quo, then I think we owe it to our descendants to at least explain how we misread the signs of the times.

Sincerely

Peter Breen

Prodigal Pilgrim Group

Pilgrim Letter 10

The Miracle of the Sun as a Portent

Prodigal Pilgrim Group

Hotel Santa Maria

R de Santo Antonio 79

Fatima, Portugal

August 25, 2019

Fr Jorge Mario Bergoglio

Holy Father Pope Francis

Papal Residence

Domus Sanctae Marthae

00120 Citta del Vatican

Dear Fr Jorge

I spent my final day in Fatima exploring the records of the last days of the Fatima apparitions and especially the terrifying Miracle of the Sun. I had the luxury of a desk and chair in the library and museums complex.

All that remained of the precious holm oak shrub on the night before the sixth and last apparition at the Cova da Iria was its trunk—faithfully adorned with flowers and ribbons by Maria de Carreira after pushing her way through the large crowd already gathered and sleeping rough in anticipation of a good position for the next day's promised miracle. Everyone was wet and muddy from intermittent rain.

Early the next day, October 13, 1917, pilgrims searched a grey sky, hoping for a fine day to witness the spectacle. At about ten in the morning, the weather closed in, and sheets of rain lashed the Cova, drenching the roads and chilling pilgrims to the bone. *Estimates of the crowd ranged from forty thousand to eighty thousand in the Cova itself. Another twenty thousand were watching from about twenty-five miles around.*[89] Lucia's mother had decided that this was her youngest daughter's last day on Earth—the day her monstrous lie would be exposed—and an angry crowd would seek vengeance. But recognizing the seriousness of the situation, Maria Rosa's tough love had softened, and she decided to be on hand, *for if my daughter dies, I want to be at her side.*[90] Lucia wrote in her memoir:

> *We left home quite early, expecting that we would be delayed along the way. Masses of people [a crowd estimated at 70,000] thronged the roads. The rain fell in torrents. My mother, her heart torn with uncertainty as to what was going to happen, and fearing it would be the last day of my life, wanted to accompany me. On the way, the scenes of the previous month, still more numerous and moving, were repeated ... We reached the holm oak in*

the Cova da Iria. Once there, moved by an interior im-
pulse, I asked the people to shut their umbrellas and say
the Rosary. A little later, we saw the flash of light, and
then Our Lady appeared on the holm oak.

> *Lucia: What do you want of me?*
>
> *Our Lady: I want to tell you that a chapel is to be built*
> *here in my honor. I am the Lady of the Rosary.*
> *Continue always to pray the Rosary every day.*
> *The war is going to end and the soldiers will re-*
> *turn to their homes.*
>
> *Lucia: I have many things to ask you: the cure of some*
> *sick persons, the conversion of sinners, and other*
> *things ...*
>
> *Our Lady: Some yes, but not others. They must amend*
> *their lives and ask forgiveness for their sins ... Do*
> *not offend the Lord our God anymore, because He*
> *is already offended.*

Then, opening her hands, she made them reflect the
sun, and as she ascended, the reflection of her own
light continued to be projected on the sun itself ...[91]

People in the immediate vicinity of the children heard
Lucia cry out: *Look at the sun.*[92] They watched in astonishment as the clouds drew back, exposing the normally fiery

ball as similar in appearance to a pale disc of mother-of-pearl, and then spinning like a fire wheel and throwing off multi-colored rays of light in all directions. After a few minutes, the solar gyrations ceased momentarily, before resuming with even greater intensity, illuminating everything on the ground with different colors. *And then as if taking on new life, it became a hurtling dynamo of incredible colors, falling everywhere like an exploding rainbow ... All at once, the sun detached itself from the sky and came plunging zig-zaggedly down on the screaming multitude like a monstrous fireball ... At the last moment, the sun arrested its death plunge and climbed back into the sky to resume its normal position and brightness.*[93]

One journalist who witnessed the solar miracle that day at the Cova da Iria was Avelino de Almeida, the editor of the government newspaper *O Seculo*, an anti-clerical publication that promised to eliminate religion within two years. Almeida described the sun as a plaque of dull silver that neither burned nor blinded the eyes. *Before the astonished eyes of the crowd ... the sun trembled, made sudden incredible movements outside all cosmic laws – the sun danced according to the typical expression of the people.* Afterwards, the journalist made notes as the people discussed what they had seen. *The great majority admitted to having seen the trembling and dancing of the sun. Others affirmed that they saw the face of the Blessed Virgin, while others swore that the sun whirled on itself like a giant catherine wheel and that it lowered itself to the earth as if to burn it with its rays.*[94]

Eyewitnesses reported seeing the miracle up to thirty miles from the Cova da Iria. An American building contractor was working eight miles from Fatima in a village near Minde. He told the writer, John Haffert, in 1960 that he saw the sun fall from the sky. *I thought it was the end of the world.*[95] The phenomenon was not recorded in any meteorological station, so remains within the realm of private revelation. Even so, for the first time in recorded history, a prophet or seer had successfully asked people to assemble in advance of a miracle *to prove that the message which had been received came from God.*[96] It was a brave call and Lucia's mother had every reason to be concerned if the promised miracle failed to materialize.

Under the protective custody of Maria de Carreira (who became known as Maria da Capelinha), a chapel was built as requested on the hollowed-out ground that once held the trunk and root system of the loved-to-death holm oak shrub. In her role as the first custodian of the shrine, Maria recorded extraordinary healings during the 1918 Spanish flu pandemic then sweeping the world. Many people arrived in Fatima that year, either suffering from the disease or fearful of catching it. A priest named Friar David from a nearby village gave the first sermon at the Cova, emphasizing that the most important prerequisite to healing was a change of life. *People were weeping in sorrow over the epi-*

demic [and] Our Lady heard the prayers they offered because from that day on, we had no more cases of influenza.[97]

Another healing story recorded by Maria da Capelinha involved a man from another village who she had found crying near one of the holm oak trees on the Cova. He had no faith at all in God or any religion —and yet had been cured of an open leg wound which had tortured him for twenty-four years. His wife insisted on praying a nine-day novena and making a poultice from dirt extracted from under the holm oak of the apparitions and rubbing it into her husband's wound. Every day for nine days she washed the wound with the mud and each day it healed a little more, until at the end of the novena it was perfectly cured.

On his first visit to the Cova, the local bishop recognized the need for water, directing Maria's husband to dig a well. During the first day of the dig, the workers hit rock, but water flowed generously when the rock was blasted. *Everyone had the greatest faith in our Lady's water, and she used it to cure their wounds and their pains. Never did our Lady perform so many miracles as at that time.*[98]

The foundation stone for the Basilica of Our Lady of the Rosary was laid on the highest point of the Cova on October 13, 1928; in 1953, the basilica was officially consecrated. Between the capelinha and the basilica, a larger holm oak where the children often sheltered as they waited for Our Lady was fenced off to protect it from the quest for amulets and healing potions. Today it towers over the capelinha, which is enclosed within the more modern Chapel of the Apparitions. Each year, the shrine welcomes up to five million visitors—the second highest tourist destination in Portugal after its capital Lisbon.

Promises of signs and wonders are not so exceptional today as they were in 1917, and it's easy to dismiss them as mass hysteria. The *sun spins and scientists are baffled* to quote John Cornwell in *Powers of Darkness Powers of Light*, a book published in 1991 when I first visited Medjugorje, at the suggestion of Marjorie Weekes in the Vatican social communications office. At the end of his book, Cornwell found pause for thought in the Marian apparitions: *For my own part, these wanderings in the milieu of popular mysticism led not to the discovery of evidence for the supernatural but to the conviction that I could no longer bask in confident unbelief.*[99] Others need no convincing, Holy Father, certainly of the veracity of the miracles at Fatima.

What I find fascinating is the symmetry between the Fatima apparitions and the apparitions of Medjugorje, where bold predictions are again being made of a miracle to prove that Mary's messages are from God. Just a few days before the first of the Fatima apparitions in May 1917, your predecessor Pope Benedict XV sent a pastoral letter asking every person of faith to pray for Mary's intercession before God as the 'Mother of Mercy' and 'Queen of Peace', to bring an end to the devastation of World War I. Similarly, in June 1981, Mary appeared at Medjugorje for the first

time—within weeks of Pope John Paul II seeking her intervention as 'Mother of all individuals and peoples', following
his near-death experience at the hands of the would-be as-
sassin in St Peter's Square. Mary affirmed to the visionaries
at Medjugorje that both apparitions—Fatima and Medjugorje—are connected to the triumph of her heart.[100]

Questions remain about the Medjugorje prophecies.
Unlike the promised miracle at Fatima, no date has been
announced for the prospective events foretold at Medjugorje. Whatever the prophetic timeline might be, some people
will believe that what they see is from God, while others will
be skeptical. Such is the nature of private revelation: one
person's irrefutable evidence is another person's seed of
doubt. Four-fifths of the space in my hotel room is occupied by dark matter which scientists know nothing about,
so we could be waiting a long time for a satisfactory scientific explanation for paranormal phenomena such as Mary's
apparitions.

I see you had firsthand experience of a paranormal
phenomenon in your former role as auxiliary bishop of
Buenos Aires when a discarded communion host from one
of your parish churches appeared to take on the physical
properties of human flesh. You sought the assistance of a
renowned scientist, Dr Ricardo Castanon Gomez, who in
turn engaged the forensic and investigative skills of two
Australians, lawyer Ron Tesoriero and television journalist
Mike Willesee. The two men travelled to Poughkeepsie on

the Hudson River, about 60 miles north of New York City, where they met former county medical examiner and heart specialist, Dr Frederick Zugibe. Zugibe pronounced his verdict after examining the communion host material on a glass slide under a medical microscope. *This flesh is heart muscle tissue, myocardium from the left ventricle wall, not far from a valvular area ... The myocardial condition was not caused by the death of a person. The slide showed no evidence of death. This sample was alive at the time it was collected.*[101] Nobody told the doctor in advance of his microscopic examination that what he was looking at was once a communion host.

Mike Willesee died a year ago and posthumously published a book which included many references to his attempts at finding a DNA profile in what he called the 'Buenos Aires communion host'. It struck me that many of us might have been satisfied with confirmation that the communion host mysteriously turned into heart muscle, without the need for further DNA testing to break *the biggest story of all – the real presence of Jesus.*[102] I had the opportunity to talk with Mike Willesee about the remarkable things he had already achieved, but the journalist remained a man on a mission to the end. He was never going to give up on his quest to prove the unprovable proposition that the God of all creation is to be found in a communion host.

At the time of his death from throat cancer, Willesee was trying to match his Buenos Aires communion host sample to dried blood from the Shroud of Turin. Lawyer Ron Tesoriero is still working on the project. *It is now certainly within the realm of possibilities to consider a human being as a 'special creation' for there exists, on multiple glass slides, human heart cells which are spontaneous special creations with no ancestry.*[103] Ron is anxious to disprove Darwin's theory of evolution—a task that is only marginally less difficult than proving the real presence.

The lawyer is hoping to obtain your permission to access what is alleged to be Jesus' burial garment— notwithstanding recent carbon dating tests which placed the origin of the shroud in the Middle Ages. Many experts claim the tests were flawed, since part of the test sample was taken from a repaired hem of the garment. Anyway, Ron Tesoriero has taken up the challenge of trying to identify the dried blood from the Shroud of Turin in a DNA match with the miraculous communion host. Apparently he is lobbying you through the Buenos Aires priest who first witnessed the eucharistic miracle, Fr Alejandro Pezet—a priest held in high esteem by the Church. You are ideally placed to comprehend the issues, Holy Father, given your role in the investigation and official report of the forensic study of the Buenos Aires communion host.

My understanding is that the Pontifical Academy of Sciences has the expertise to supervise further forensic tests of the communion host and compare the results with the dried blood of the burial garment, although there is no expectation that you will find any male DNA, given the extensive search for genetic markers already undertaken on the communion host. No surprise to me that the Holy Spirit has no DNA profile, but there is always the prospect of identifying Mary's matriarchal heritage of Jesus in the mitochondrial DNA, a project Ron Tesoriero has worked on for the past thirty years.

And now, Holy Father, I am signing off from Fatima, with the bus due to depart first thing tomorrow morning for the next stage of my pilgrimage. I will be walking on eggshells when I reach the little village of San Sebastian de Garabandal in the Cantabrian Mountains region of northern Spain, since Mary's apparitions in that neck of the woods have not been approved by the Church. Some commentators say that Garabandal has already failed the 'worthy of belief' test for Marian apparitions, as determined by the Congregation for the Doctrine of the Faith, while others say Mary appeared on the hill above the village, but the devil overwhelmed the young visionaries. As always, it's not my role to pass judgment on these things, merely to check in with you as to what is going on in the Church, and hopefully to renew my faith. The devil thing is always tricky, as it raises the thorny issue of human sin and who ultimately bears responsibility for our bad behavior.

I do hope you will continue to indulge me with any interest you may have in my pilgrimage, which at this point is halfway along the road to finding out what Mary's triumph and peace on Earth might look like.

Sincerely
Peter Breen
Prodigal Pilgrim Group

Part Three

The Promises of Garabandal
1961-1965

Pilgrim Letter 11

A Precarious Appearance in the Mountains

Prodigal Pilgrim Group
Hosteria Garabandal
San Sebastian de Garabandal
Cantabria, Spain

September 2, 2019

Fr Jorge Mario Bergoglio
Holy Father Pope Francis
Papal Residence
Domus Sanctae Marthae
00120 Citta del Vaticano

Dear Fr Jorge

The long bus trip from Fatima in Portugal to the Cantabrian Mountains in the north of Spain—with a stopover for lunch in Salamanca—turned out to be a tough day at the office. It was especially so at the end, as we threaded our way up the narrow bitumen road through the Pena Sagra mountain range, finally reaching the village of Garabandal just on dusk. At the end of the trip, the bus driver managed to jam the undercarriage of the bus on the Garabandal hotel's steep driveway. One by one the passengers alighted, giving the bus just enough lift for the driver to reverse clear of the driveway and park on the concrete pavement in front of the adjoining restaurant, where we had dinner. Next morning, it took less than an hour to explore the village, which consisted of half a dozen commercial buildings, about 60 houses, a church, cemetery and two or three religious gift shops. Nothing much had changed in Garabandal since the last of the Marian apparitions in November 1965.

One of the American pilgrims, Penny, introduced me to the director of the Pilgrim Center in the village, a man named Michael from Philadelphia, who attended Penn State University and held degrees in philosophy and theology from St Charles Borromeo Seminary in Wynnewood, Pennsylvania. Michael showed a short film, informing us that an angel appeared to four young girls in the village followed by a series of apparitions of Mary, beginning on July 2, 1961, and concluding on November 13, 1965. The youthful visionaries were Maria Concepción (Conchita) González, Marí Dolores (Loli) Mazón, Jacinta González (all aged 12 years) and Marí Cruz González (aged 11 years).

Conchita kept a diary, which included an entry recording the first day Mary appeared on a goat track called the Calleja leading up to a stand of fir trees ('the Pines') on a hill behind the village. According to Conchita's diary, Mary appeared wearing *a white dress, a blue mantle and a crown of small golden stars.*[104] The diary is published in full within another book by an American priest, who discounted the possibility that the four witnesses were experiencing hallucinatory phenomena. *A person suffering from hallucination has only vague and hazy recollections. The forms that he [she] sees are vaporous and indeterminate. Also, the writings of the hallucinated are characterized by incomprehensible sentences, incomplete lines, unfinished words, incoherent citations and prophecies etc. Although 'Conchita's Diary' is a very simple and unsophisticated document, it is quite free from these vagaries.* [105] Vagaries may be absent from the diary, but enough of them persist in other aspects of the apparitions to suggest the Church is struggling to find them 'worthy of belief'.

Prominent among the vagaries is the difficult location of Garabandal with one narrow road from the south and another from the north providing the only access to the isolated village and its precarious plateau. Mary could not have picked a worse place for pilgrimage if she hoped to replicate Lourdes and Fatima, given the logistical problems of accommodating large numbers of visitors in a remote mountain region. Another vagary is the extraordinary way the child visionaries behaved during their apparitions, which I will talk about in another letter. Perhaps the biggest problem though is the lack of Church support for the Garabandal messages, which reflected badly on the clergy of the 1960s —even though the messages seem to be right on the money in the context of the sex abuse crimes perpetrated under Church protection.

Garabandal's first message, communicated to the four girls as they walked up the Calleja towards the Pines on July 2, 1961 (publicly revealed on October 18, 1961), was recorded in Conchita's diary. *The Blessed Virgin was smiling as usual ... Then she told us we must make many sacrifices, perform much penance and visit the Blessed Sacrament. But first, we must lead very good lives – ser muy Buenos. If we do not, a chastisement will befall us. The cup is already filling up, and if we do not change, a very great chastisement will come upon us.*[106]

As you know, Holy Father, this message is entirely consistent with the messages of Lourdes and Fatima—prayer, penance, fasting and conversion, meaning a change of heart and turning away from sin. More controversial is the second message given to Conchita on June 18, 1965, a message also recorded in her diary—this time in the present tense, and using Mary's direct first-person speech.

As my message of October 18 [1961] has not been complied with and has not been made known to the world, I am advising you that this is the last one. Before, the cup was filling up. Now it is overflowing. Many cardinals, many bishops and many priests are on the road to perdition and are taking many souls with them. Less and less importance is being given to the Eucharist. You should turn the wrath of God away from yourselves by your efforts. If you ask him for-giveness with sincere hearts, he will pardon you. I, your Mother, through the intercession of Saint Michael the archangel, ask you to amend your lives. You are now receiving the last warnings. I love you and do not want your condemnation. Pray to us with sincerity and we will grant your requests. You should make more sacri-fices. Think about the passion of Jesus.[107]

At the end of the short film about the Garabandal appa-ritions, I watched dispassionately as Michael made his pitch to the pilgrims. Dressed in khaki chinos, matching baseball cap and long sleeve fire engine red polo shirt, Michael spoke confidently about the parallels between the messages of Garabandal and the secrets of Fatima. He quoted Bishop Joao Venancio, a former bishop of Leiria-Fatima, as saying in 1983 that the *message given by the Most Holy Virgin in Garabandal is the same that She gave in Fatima, but it is updated for our time.*[108] Venancio was privy to Fatima's third secret and Michael quoted the bishop in support of the proposition that the secret was not fully revealed in the year 2000. Michael also quoted an advisor to Pope John XXIII who read the secret and suggested that the messages of Garabandal were a repetition of Fatima's third secret in brief form.

After his pitch, I chatted with Michael about his extensive research work on the Fatima secrets. I explained that I was working on a submission to the vice-postulator of the cause for the canonization of Sr Lucia. I was also hopeful of an interview with the main Garabandal visionary, Conchita González, who was a good friend of one of the American pilgrims, 'Rosey' (not her real name). Rosey was full of praise for the visionary, telling me that Conchita had just turned 70 after devoting her adult life to her husband of 40 years, Patrick Keena, until his untimely death in 2013. These days, Conchita enjoyed relative obscurity, spending much of her time with her four children and fifteen grandchildren. (Marí Loli Mazón died in New Hampshire, USA, in 2009 and is survived by her husband and three of her four children. Jacinta González married and moved to the USA. She lives with her husband and daughter in California. Marí Cruz González also married and lives in Spain with her husband and four children).

Michael gave me a series of questions for Conchita about her meetings with Sr Lucia, Bishop Venancio and the saintly Capuchin priest, Padre Pio. The purpose of the questions was to build on the thesis that the third secret of Fatima and the messages of Garabandal were all part of the same prophecy—the triumph of Mary's heart and a period of peace. While I had little interest in revisiting the third secret of Fatima, nonetheless I was fascinated to hear Michael expounding on the idea that Mary appeared at Garabandal *after Sr Lucia was silenced and the third secret of Fatima was hidden.*[109] Michael had worked out that Mary delivered the first message at Garabandal five months and 20 days before convocation of the Second Vatican Ecumenical Council in 1961. And the second message was delivered in 1965, exactly five months and 20 days before the Council ended on December 8—the feast day of Mary's Immaculate Conception. Nothing turned on the symmetry, although an inference can be drawn that Mary was somehow bookending Vatican II, as a strategy to limit its influence on the Church.

I left Michael to catch up with the American pilgrims, who were halfway along the Calleja track that twisted and turned up the hill to the Pines. I passed a recess in the stone wall on one side of the track where a small shrine marked the place Mary had first appeared to the young visionaries. On the back wall of the shrine, a painting depicted Mary as the girls had described her—white dress, blue mantle, long brown wavy hair, parted in the middle, the brown scapular on her right wrist. The depiction is that of Our Lady of Mount Carmel. Reaching the top of the hill, I rested with our group in the shade of the Pines—the place where Mary promised a miracle to prove the apparitions were from God. We posed for a group photograph in front of the largest of the pine trees, as the photographer adjusted the picture to include the life-size statue of the Mount Carmel image perched high in the branches.

It was there at the Pines on January 1, 1965 that Mary appeared in apparition and promised 'the Warning' which would precede 'the Great Miracle', to be followed by 'the Great Chastisement' if the world did not change its sinful ways. Writing in her diary, Conchita said that the Warning *will be visible all over the world*.[110] In a letter written on the day after the apparition, Conchita said that the purpose of the Warning was to give people the opportunity to change their lives and draw closer to God, thereby enabling them to be more amenable to the Great Miracle. If people did not amend their lives, then the Great Chastisement would follow. While the Warning would disappear after engaging the consciousness of every person alive, the Great Miracle would include a visible, permanent, and untouchable sign at the Pines.

Do not stop reading now, Holy Father—the young visionaries could not make up this stuff! Besides, the promise of a visible, permanent, and untouchable sign has never been made since Marian apparitions began in the year 40 CE—when Mary appeared to James the Apostle in Spain—other than at Medjugorje in 1981. In my correspondence, there must be at least the possibility that the mysterious sign promised at Garabandal is the same sign prophesied at Medjugorje. As well as the possibility of sharing the same sign—the same Great Miracle—Medjugorje and Garabandal may also be sharing the same Warning and the same

Great Chastisement if the pilgrims I am travelling with are to be believed.

In case you are wondering, I did look around at the Pines and questioned what kind of sign with worldwide significance might appear in such a small space, barely the size of an Australian Rules football field. If the promised sign appears as a natural phenomenon, the odds seem to favor fire, air, water, or earth—or maybe a combination of all four elements of matter. My guess is Moses' burning bush revisited, since fire is the only element we cannot touch without consequences. Or maybe the sign will be some untouchable and otherworldly form of light, such as surrounds Marian apparitions.

Let me know if you think all this is just a bit incongruous, Holy Father. I do understand that any promise of signs from God is not everyone's cup of tea. If you are interested in how the signs of the times might work in practice, consider Australia's Aboriginal people—the oldest surviving culture on Earth—who seamlessly integrate the natural and spiritual worlds.

Anyway, I ask that you also consider the possibility of an official recognition of pilgrimages to the Garabandal shrine, with the same enthusiasm you showed recently for pilgrimages to Medjugorje. In my opinion, the Church has been tough on the Garabandal visionaries for having the courage to speak out about perverse members of the clergy. Perhaps you are concerned about a 1966 report to the effect that the visionary, Conchita González, had a meeting with Pope Paul VI, and afterwards described him in unflattering terms. *The Pope gave me the impression of being an oppressed person, as if restrained by the cardinals and the hierarchy.* [111]

Conchita was just seventeen years young at the time and should be forgiven for something said in private that the child could never have imagined would be reported. The same report included Conchita's infamous statement that after Pope Paul VI there would be just two more popes before the end of the times. It's now generally agreed that Conchita's reference to the end of the times was intended to describe a certain period in human history, which marked the end of the time leading up to the Warning, the Great Miracle, and the Great Chastisement. Who can say with confidence, Holy Father, that we are not already in that time?

An alternative interpretation is that fulfillment of the Garabandal promises will mark the end of the times. Here are Conchita's words as reported in 1966: *I asked the Virgin, 'Will the end of the world be during the time of these future happenings?' She answered me, 'No, the end of the times.'* [112] Then followed Conchita's controversial words about the number of popes: *After Paul VI there will only be two more popes; and after that the end of the times.* Counting popes can be tricky when one lasts just 33 days, a second survives a bullet wound that might have been fatal to other mere mortals and a third unexpectedly retires. If we are now in the time leading up to the Warning, the Great Miracle, and the Great Chastisement, I would argue that it began with your papacy and its clarion call to protect the natural environment.[113]

If I were you, Holy Father, I would not place too much emphasis on an unreliable report from a private conversation in 1966, when Conchita expected to be entering the convent. Rather, I would consider further examination of Garabandal's promises through a properly constituted and official Vatican inquiry, before finally deciding whether the Marian apparitions that shadowed the Second Vatican Ecumenical Council are 'worthy of belief'. To assist you in your deliberations, I will respectfully devote the next three letters to each of the three promised Garabandal signs—the Warning, the Great Miracle, and the Great Chastisement.

Sincerely

Peter Breen

Prodigal Pilgrim Group

Pilgrim Letter 12

The Warning—Visible around the World

Prodigal Pilgrim Group
Hosteria Garabandal
San Sebastian de Garabandal
Cantabria, Spain

September 9, 2019

Fr Jorge Mario Bergoglio
Holy Father Pope Francis
Papal Residence
Domus Sanctae Marthae
00120 Citta del Vaticano

Dear Fr Jorge

It's hard to beat bad luck, but just as I was about to write to you, I received a long email (11 printed pages) about the Warning in the form of a chain letter, which was circulated by a well-meaning pious Catholic, and signed 'Your beloved Jesus'. May the saints preserve us, Holy Father! I think it was Mahatma Gandhi who said he would be a follower of Christ, were it not for the Christians.

I emailed the original source of the chain letter, to find out who was the privileged recipient of a private revelation in the form of an email from Jesus. I learned that the chain letter originated from an Irish prayer group on the fringes of the Catholic Church. Members of the group claimed to be heralding the Second Coming of Jesus (not to be confused with a Second Pentecost), while promoting the notion that *Bergoglio is the False Prophet of the Apocalypse … who is destroying our Church right before our eyes and preparing for the Antichrist to sit in Peter's chair in the Vatican.*[114] Oh dear! A good rule of thumb is not to engage with anyone who claims to have a role to play in the Second Coming of Jesus or believes that the Antichrist will manifest within Catholic Church governance.

Meanwhile, the chain letter reminded me that the Church teaches—for good reason—that nobody is obliged to believe in any form of private revelation, including private revelations approved by the Church.[115] Even so, Church approval does lend a certain level of credibility to Mary's apparitions. Garabandal has suffered from the absence of the Church's stamp of approval. Bishop Doreto Fernandez, the apostolic administrator of the diocese of Santander, which includes Garabandal, decided as early as 1961 that: *Nothing up to the present obliges us to affirm that the events are supernatural.* Then the bishop held two further inquiries which reached the same conclusion.[116]

Surely the inquiries were premature? At Lourdes and Fatima, for example, the Church waited for the apparitions to conclude, before speaking out officially on the character of what had occurred. A Vatican commission of inquiry (the Ruini report) has been established at Medjugorje—even though the apparitions are ongoing. Would you consider a Vatican commission of inquiry for Garabandal?

Such a discrete inquiry into the early appearances of Mary at the Calleja and the Pines might have a comparable outcome to the Medjugorje inquiry, which was a huge vote of confidence for supporters, and bolstered the number of pilgrims visiting Medjugorje. Of course, you may want to see whether any prophecies from the Garabandal apparitions come to pass. But all the Medjugorje prophecies remain unfulfilled (as do some of the Fatima prophecies), and the Medjugorje commission seemed to be unfazed by that circumstance.

So why would a Garabandal inquiry be concerned about how future events might unfold? If you do not give at least tentative recognition to the Garabandal apparitions through a discrete inquiry, there is a risk that supporters will become marginalized, and the object of their prayer and devotion turned into an anomaly—or worse, labeled as devil worship.

For a modern perspective on the Garabandal revelations about the Warning, Holy Father, may I recommend a recent book of the same name. It has received wide acclaim, including from eminent theologian Dr Mark Miravalle, who said in an endorsement at the front of the text that the Warning *is substantially confirmed within the church's mystical tradition, as well as through numerous contemporary prophetic voices within the church.*[117] The young Garabandal visionaries are generally included in any list of credible modern prophets and three of them are quoted in the book:

> *Conchita: If I did not know about the other chastisement to come, I would say there is no greater chastisement than the Warning ... It will be visible in every part of the world, no matter where we live ... Believers as well as unbelievers, wherever they are at the time, will see and feel it ... It will be like fire; it will not burn our flesh, but we will feel it corporeally and interiorly. All nations and every person on earth will feel it. No one shall escape it. And unbelievers will feel the fear of God ... The most important thing about that day is that everyone in the whole world will see a sign, a grace, or a punishment within themselves. They will find themselves all alone in the world, no matter where they are at the time, alone with their consciences right before God ...*

Mari Loli: It will be an interior personal experience. It will look as if the world had come to a standstill, however, no one will be aware of that as they will be totally absorbed in their own experience ... often when we do something wrong, we just ask with our lips for the Lord to forgive us, but now, He will help us sense that deep sorrow ...

Jacinta: The Warning is something that is just seen in the air, everywhere in the world, and immediately is transmitted into the interior of our souls. It will last for a very little time, but it will seem a very long time because of its effects within us. It will be good for our souls, in order to see in ourselves our conscience – the good that we have failed to do, and the bad we have done. [118]

Other modern spiritual writers tell us that before the Great Chastisement, God in his mercy will provide us with the opportunity to make amends for our willful errors and misdeeds. *This moment in which we see ourselves as God sees us is popularly known as the 'Warning'. It will be a supernatural occurrence associated with an event in the sky that will cause every man, woman and child to see the state of his or her own soul.* [119]

Any list of modern mystics will include Sr Faustina Kowalska [1905-1938] who was canonized by your predecessor, Pope John Paul II, in the year 2000. During the canonization ceremony, the pope described Sr Faustina as the Great Apostle of Divine Mercy in our time. Her conversations with Jesus are recorded in her diary, which was published following her canonization. The saintly nun wrote about a universal illumination of conscience. *Before the day of justice arrives, [a] sign in the sky will be given to mankind [in the form of the Cross of Jesus]. All light in the heavens will be extinguished, and there will be great darkness over the whole earth.*[120] Sr Faustina experienced her own illumination of conscience, which she described in her diary. *Suddenly, I saw the complete condition of my soul as God sees it.*[121]

Some prophetic voices say that the Warning will take place when two celestial bodies collide, *lighting up the entire earth [so that] the day will be brighter and the night will be like the day.*[122] No surprise that the saints have different perceptions of God's mercy—as different as night and day. What they do agree on is that the Warning starts out as a sign in the sky visible around the world, a sign that God uses to speak interiorly to every person on Earth. Good people will be drawn nearer to God; sinners will have an opportunity to amend their lives.

Conchita explained that the Warning is *like two stars that crash and make a lot of noise and a lot of light but they don't fall.* Then follows what Mari Loli called *a big silence, like a sense of emptiness.*[123] Alone of the visionaries, Mari Loli knew the year of the Warning, but she took the information to her grave in 2009. She did say that the Warning would occur during the 12 months preceding the Great Miracle, and Conchita knows the date of the miracle. Various attempts to extract the date from Conchita (including death threats) have failed. The most she will say is *I can't reveal it until eight days before the date.*[124]

My pilgrim colleague, Rosey, assured me that Conchita is a saintly woman and a trustworthy custodian of the Garabandal prophecies. During the apparition on January 1, 1965, when the young visionary learned about the Warning, she was invited to unite her earthly suffering with Jesus' passion and death. Like the children at Fatima, Conchita bravely accepted the prospect of suffering without knowing what she was signing up for. The young visionary could not have imagined the self-doubt and harassment she was destined to encounter when the Garabandal apparitions were mostly received with incredulity. I will tell you more of Conchita's troubles in the next couple of letters.

I might not have taken you through the detail of an unapproved series of Mary's apparitions were it not for the similarities between Garabandal's promises and the signs of Medjugorje. Assuming I still have your attention this far down the track, Holy Father, the next thing I would like to do is examine in more detail Garabandal's promised Great Miracle which includes a visible and permanent sign that may bear a striking resemblance to the visible and perma-

nent sign prophesied to the children at Medjugorje—
generally known as Medjugorje's third secret.

Sincerely
Peter Breen
Prodigal Pilgrim Group

Pilgrim Letter 13

The Great Miracle—Visible in the Mountains

Prodigal Pilgrim Group

Hosteria Garabandal

San Sebastian de Garabandal

Cantabria, Spain

September 14, 2019

Fr Jorge Mario Bergoglio

Holy Father Pope Francis

Papal Residence

Domus Sanctae Marthae

00120 Citta del Vaticano

Dear Fr Jorge

I have no way of knowing if my letters are getting though the front door of the Domus Sanctae Marthae, let alone whether you are reading them. You probably receive correspondence by the truckload! Anyway, I am inclined to press on, since you asked what the faithful think, and writing letters is good work if you can get it.

As to the promised Great Miracle of Garabandal, Conchita said it would be visible in the village and from the surrounding mountains. *There won't be the slightest doubt that it comes from God and that it is for the good of mankind. A sign of the miracle, which it will be possible to film or televise, will remain forever at the pines.*[125] Apparently the Great Miracle will be an extraordinary supernatural event that will leave a visible and permanent sign from out of this world.

Before writing anything further about the Great Miracle, I took the liberty of consulting CS Lewis' book on miracles, and I was reminded that the word 'miracle' is used to mean an interference with nature by supernatural power. *Unless there exists in addition to nature, something else that we may call the supernatural, there can be no miracles.*[126] With one or two exceptions, the miracles of Scripture are nature miracles, although sometimes a distinction is drawn between nature miracles and the healing miracles. If God intervenes in nature, *Nature merely domiciles this new situation, makes it at home in her realm [and] adapts all other events to it.*[127] Changing water into wine is not unnatural. Neither is multiplying the loaves and fishes or healing the sick in my correspondence. God simply facilitates shortcuts in nature. Even the miracle of the real presence in the Bueno Aries communion host, for example, is consistent with nature, in the sense that much of the inanimate food we eat eventually becomes flesh and blood.

In a similar vein, virgin birth and walking on water are not unheard of in nature. Life, death, and resurrection itself in various forms occur in nature without any leap of faith or further explanation being necessary, other than admitting the possibility of the hand of God in something that is otherwise inexplicable. Of course, many aspects of nature remain hidden, or rather are incomprehensible to the ordinary mind, so God works with the laws of nature—including with the laws we are yet to comprehend.

The main exception to the nature miracles asserted by Christianity is what Lewis called the Grand Miracle—God became man. This Miracle of the Incarnation must be in a category of its own, since every other Christian miracle is a quirk of nature, or a hybrid of something already occurring in nature. While we recognise the possibility of the invasion of nature by the supernatural, the invasion of humanity by God is something quite different. But how different is it? If the Grand Miracle is accepted, it *illuminates and orders all other phenomena, explains both our laughter and our logic, our fear of the dead and our knowledge that it is somehow good to die, and which at one stroke covers what multitudes of separate theories will hardly cover.* [128]

A question arises as to whether Garabandal's Great Miracle and the Warning will be in that elite class of miracles—like the Grand Miracle—beyond nature. None of the seers at Garabandal has seen the Great Miracle, although it was described in detail to Mari Loli and Conchita. Conchita referred to the miracle as completely different to that of

Fatima, *a miracle of the love of God that will prove and manifest his love to us in an outstanding way.*[129]

The only person to have seen the Great Miracle (other than Padre Pio) was Jesuit priest Fr Luis Andreu who died the same day. Conchita described what happened in an interview:

> *Question: Can you tell us something about Fr Luis Andreu?*
>
> *Conchita: Yes, this priest came frequently to the village to see if the apparitions were real or not. After a while he believed in them. Once, while we were in ecstasy at the pines, he began to shout, "Miracle, miracle, miracle." When this happened, the Virgin said: "At this moment the priest is seeing me and the Miracle that will occur."*
>
> *Question: Fr Luis was actually seeing the Miracle?*
>
> *Conchita: Yes. That same day on his trip back home he said to his friends, "This is the happiest day of my life. What a great mother we have in heaven. The apparitions are true." As he said these words he died.*
>
> *Question: Didn't the Virgin say something would occur on the day of the Miracle concerning Fr Andreu?*
>
> *Conchita: Yes, she said on the day of the Miracle that his body would be found incorrupt (Conchita*

clarified that the exhumation would occur the day after the Miracle). [130]

Luis Andreu and his brother Ramon were both Jesuit priests who visited Garabandal in the early days of the apparitions. They took notes, observed the visionaries in ecstasy and spoke with other witnesses. It so happened that on August 8, 1961, the parish priest of Garabandal had to leave the village on business for the day and he left Fr Luis Andreu in charge. The Jesuit priest said morning Mass in the parish church and the villagers present included the four young visionaries. Early in the afternoon, the girls received an apparition in the church, causing them to fall into an ecstatic state. Just before 9:00pm following evening prayers in the church, the girls were again found to be in a state of ecstasy in front of the main altar, as they prayed to the Lady of Mount Carmel. Conchita was heard to say to the supernatural visitor: *But we haven't given any proof and the people don't believe.* [131] At around 9:40pm, the four girls left the church in an ecstatic march which took them up the Calleja to the Pines.

Fr Luis knelt in the vicinity of the girls at the Pines, as they continued in their rapturous conversation with the Lady. Normally they would be unaware of others during their ecstasy, but they could see Fr Luis looking up towards the apparition. They heard him repeat the word 'miracle'. In her diary, Conchita said: *We could see him. Now, in our*

ecstasies we never saw anyone (except the Blessed Virgin).
But we saw Fr Luis and the Blessed Virgin told us that he
was seeing her and the miracle too.[132]

Sometime after 10:00pm when the apparition concluded, Fr Luis was given a lift in a jeep to Cosio where he trans-
ferred to a passenger vehicle—one of five vehicles travelling
in convoy—for the journey home to Aguilar de Campo.
Along the way he said he felt sleepy, before lowering his
head and dying. Fr Luis was driven to a nearby hospital
where he was officially pronounced dead. He was 36 years
old, physically strong, and active, and he had no known
health problems. He is buried in the church cemetery at
Ona, where he was professor of theology at the local Jesuit
college.

Another curious feature of the Garabandal apparitions
was the fate of Joey Lomangino, the blind New York man
and inspirational supporter of the visionaries. He was a
generous benefactor, who established the Saint Anne's
Home for the Afflicted in 1964 and later the Workers of
Our Lady of Mount Carmel Center in Lindenhurst, NY.
Joey first traveled on pilgrimage to Garabandal in 1962 at
the suggestion of Padre Pio, who never doubted that Our
Lady was appearing to the four girls in the Cantabrian
Mountains village. Following his second visit in 1964, Joey
received a letter from Conchita informing him that Mary
spoke to her in locution at the Pines, to say that his sight
would be restored on the day of the Great Miracle. Conchi-

ta wrote further details on the back of a holy card she sent him, quoting Mary's direct speech: *The first thing he shall see will be the miracle, which my Son will perform through my intercession, and from that time on he will see permanently.* [133]

As you know, Holy Father, Joey Lomangino died on June 18, 2014, aged 86 years, without apparently regaining his eyesight in this life. You will be considering that fact is a minus for Church approval to the Garabandal apparitions. But June 18, 1961, was the date of the first supernatural appearance at Garabandal and June 18, 1965, the date of the last. And who can say whether Joey did get to see the Great Miracle—either before or after he died? Mary's words are not constrained by time.

Also consider Padre Pio's experience. Conchita was told in apparition that Padre Pio would see the Great Miracle before his death, but the prophecy seemed to be unfulfilled when the Capuchin priest died on September 23, 1968. Garabandal supporters were dismayed. Less than a month later, Conchita traveled to Lourdes where she met a contemporary of Padre Pio, the Italian Capuchin, Bernardino Cennamo, who presented several gifts on behalf of Padre Pio, including a handwritten message. Conchita was assured that the saintly priest did in fact see the Great Miracle before he died. *He told us himself* said Fr Bernardino when Conchita questioned him. [134]

The last thing I would like to present in support of my request that you consider a Vatican commission of inquiry into the Garabandal apparitions is the serendipity between the Garabandal promises and the Medjugorje secrets. Yes, I know the Vatican draws a distinction between the first seven Medjugorje apparitions and subsequent events, but from the very beginning the visionaries at Medjugorje asked Mary to give a sign that others might believe. In July 1981, just days after the Medjugorje apparitions began, the visionaries first disclosed that Mary *was giving them secret information concerning the future.*[135] My contention is that three of Medjugorje's secrets seem to mirror the Warning, the Great Miracle and the Great Chastisement revealed to the children at Garabandal. Perhaps the order of the secrets and the detail of the revelations will be different, but I contend we are talking about the same events, Holy Father, which could hardly be coincidental.

First, speculation is rife that Garabandal's Warning is identical to one of the Medjugorje secrets. Both involve the 'Illumination of the Soul' prophesied by the saints and spiritual leaders since the early days of Christianity. Secondly, a chastisement in the form of major disturbance in the world was also prophesied at Medjugorje. Thirdly, as I mentioned at the end of my last letter, Medjugorje's third secret appears to be the same or a comparable event to the Great Miracle of Garabandal with the promise afterwards of a visible and permanent sign to remind us of God's exceptional graces. *Everyone will be able to see that human hands could not have made [the sign].*[136]

Unlike the Warning and the Great Chastisement, we do not know much about Garabandal's Great Miracle. We know from Conchita that it will heal the sick and convert sinners who happen to be in the village (and in the surrounding mountains) on the day. Neither religion nor disease will be an obstacle to healing, but you will need to be there—covering both travel and accommodation expenses. Similarly, if you want to see the visible and permanent sign that follows the Great Miracle, rather than rely on pictures, then you will require the physical and financial resources to make the journey. I regret to say that even God's exceptional graces are likely to conspire against the poor.

In my next letter, Holy Father, I will report from Garabandal on the Great Chastisement—an event of the ages—which seems to bear a striking resemblance to the last of the Medjugorje prophecies.

Sincerely

Peter Breen

Prodigal Pilgrim Group

Pilgrim Letter 14

The Great Chastisement—Visible from Space?

Prodigal Pilgrim Group
Hosteria Garabandal
San Sebastian de Garabandal
Cantabria, Spain

September 19, 2019

Fr Jorge Mario Bergoglio
Holy Father Pope Francis
Papal Residence
Domus Sanctae Marthae
00120 Citta del Vaticano

Dear Fr Jorge

If the lack of information concerning Garabandal's Great Miracle has been troubling you, then you will be pleased to know that the prophecy of a Great Chastisement has the opposite problem—too much information. Visitors as well as Garabandal locals first heard about the Great Chastisement during the nights of June 19 and 20, 1962, in what became known as the Nights of Screams. On the first night, Mari Loli and Jacinta were visited by an angel and told to

go alone to the Pines. *As they were nearing the southern limits of the village, the girls advised the villagers ... not to advance any further ... A short while later, the girls were heard
shrieking in terror.*[137] After about 50 minutes, they came
down the hill to where the terrified crowd was waiting.
They were seen to be waving their hands in the air *as
though they were trying to ward off some frightening dan-
ger.*[138]

Mari Loli later reported what the girls witnessed:

*[Our Lady] showed us how the great Chastisement for all
mankind would come, and that it would come directly
from God ... [at a certain moment] when all motors and
machines will stop; a terrible wave of heat will strike the
earth and men will begin to feel a great thirst. In despera-
tion they will seek water, but this will evaporate from the
heat ... Then almost everyone will despair and they will
seek to kill one another ... But they will lose their
strength [and] it will be understood that it is God alone
who has permitted this.*[139]

Conchita joined the other two girls the following evening. Again, villagers and visitors were asked not to encroach
on the area in the vicinity of the Pines. To everyone's horror, the shrieks, and cries of torment of the previous evening were repeated, but much worse, lasting until two in the
morning. Some family members had to be restrained from

interfering with the apparition. Again, it was Mari Loli who reported what the girls witnessed: a crowd of people trying to escape destructive fire. *The people ran to hurl themselves into the lakes and seas. But the water seemed to boil and [instead] of putting out the flames, it seemed to enkindle them even more. It was so horrible that I asked the Most Holy Virgin to take all the young children with her before all this happened. But the Virgin told us that when it would come, they would all be adults.* [140]

Many disturbing issues are raised by these prophesies of a Great Chastisement, not the least of which is their potential relevance for today. In Australia, half the Great Barrier Reef has died due to heat stress, and each year land temperatures continue to rise as water supplies fall below critical levels. Damaging bushfires often consume electronic and communication networks. Like the prophecy that many cardinals, bishops, and priests are on the road to perdition, the idea that heat, fire, and lack of water could destroy us is not as fanciful today as it might have been 50 years ago.

I would be having another look at Garabandal if I were you, Holy Father, in the new enlightenment of the child sex abuse scandal in the Church, and the multiple ecological crises in the world.

Of course, what's lacking in the Garabandal prophecies of the Great Chastisement is the direct speech of Mary, such as Sr Lucia reported in the second secret of Fatima, where Mary prophesied in her own words the end of one world war and the beginning of another, the conversion of Russia and a period of peace in the world. At Garabandal, we do have Mary's direct words in the prophecy about many clergy members being on the road to perdition; but the promised Warning, Great Miracle and Great Chastisement are all reported in the words of the seers. And in the case of the Great Chastisement, we have virtually no words from the principal seer, Conchita, about the vision itself, other than to say that what she saw was *terrible* and *I felt a very great fear ... notwithstanding I was [also] looking at the Blessed Virgin.*[141]

One of the few times Conchita used Mary's direct speech was when the young visionary reported Mary saying that although she, Conchita, would not be happy on Earth, *you will be happy in heaven.*[142] I was curious enough about this prophecy to put it on my list of questions to ask Conchita, if I ever succeeded in catching up with her in New York. At the same time, I really was reluctant to add to her suffering after reading John Cornwell's withering interrogation of the woman in 1987 (Conchita was 38 years of age) at her home in New York.[143]

On six occasions, Conchita had refused Cornwell's telephone requests for an interview, and when he stood at the screen door of her house, she repeated that *I don't give interviews.* Eventually the writer wheedled his way inside and confronted the saintly woman, who offered him a seat in her living room. She sat opposite him, bracing herself for his questions. The first was about her life in New York, and the second went to the perplexing issue of denial. *For a time, you dismissed your visions. Why did you do that?* Conchita explained that the Bishop of Santander questioned her for hours, until she told him that she did not believe in the apparitions anymore. That was the news His Lordship wanted to hear. *He gave me absolution and forbade me to talk of them again. Then when I got back to Garabandal I felt that I had betrayed the Blessed Mother. I believed in the visions, and yet I couldn't understand how they occurred. I was torn in two.*[144]

John Cornwell is a brilliant writer, capturing Conchita's suffering as well as her attention. He asked if she was still expecting the Warning and the Great Miracle. *I'm not sure about anything anymore. Everything is against Garabandal – the bishops, the Church; all sorts of people abuse me. They tell me I'm a liar and a fake.* Cornwell's response was another question: *So now you think that you were mistaken about your visions?* Her frustration leaps off the page. *What I am telling you is that I saw a beautiful lady who told me she was the Blessed Mother. I saw her almost every day for four years. If this turns out to be false, then nothing is true. Do you understand what I'm saying? I mean nothing whatsoever is true.*[145]

Even then, the writer was not about to let his quarry off the hook, asking her whether she might have been suffering from delusions at the time of the apparitions. She spoke about the psychiatrists and psychologists who had conducted tests at the time and found all the girls were quite normal. He asked about the bizarre behavior of the girls during the apparitions, and particularly whether Conchita remembered levitating during one ecstatic episode. Her answer could not have been more credible. *Look, when the Blessed Mother came she always appeared out of a bright light; I just wasn't aware of anything else, or anybody else outside the light. And I wasn't aware of the way I was behaving.* For good measure, the writer asked Conchita what she would do if the Great Miracle does not happen, to which she replied: *That's what I'm telling you, Mister. If the miracle doesn't come, then nothing is true. What more can I say?*[146] The interrogation might have continued were it not for Conchita standing up and telling the writer he had to go. As he left, she asked him to pray for her.

Many of us pray, Holy Father, that Conchita will have the benefit of a proper inquiry into the Garabandal apparitions. The fact that she still receives death threats at age 70 is appalling and quite beyond the pale in my correspondence. If Conchita is not to have a fair and objective inquiry conducted by the local bishop, then perhaps you would consider a Vatican commission of inquiry, along the lines of the Medjugorje investigation? While it may be true that nothing turns on Church approval of the apparitions—nobody is obliged to believe any private revelation—there is a certain incongruity in the Church approving a difficult and highly controversial apparition such as La Salette in France (one appearance of Our Lady on one day in 1846), at the same time ignoring Garabandal—almost 2,000 appearances over four years.

The two young visionaries at La Salette, Melanie Calvat and Maximin Giraud, suffered terribly for what they had witnessed, both leading tragic and dysfunctional lives as they attempted to flee their interrogators. Most incredibly, Melanie changed Our Lady's public message—after Church approval in 1851—from a local famine as punishment for regional sinfulness to a general chastisement of humanity. Perhaps she was working on the Australian penal colony principle that you might as well be hung for a sheep as a lamb?

Today, nothing turns on the La Salette prophecies in my humble opinion, other than to say they cast doubt on the efficacy of Church approval as an assurance that a specific apparition of Our Lady is 'worthy of belief'. No disrespect, Holy Father, but these days the Church has higher standards of proof.

A few words, if I may, about the behavior of the four girls at Garabandal during their encounters with the Marian apparitions—a cause for consternation amongst Garabandal critics. From the very beginning of the apparitions on June 18, 1961, the girls' heads snapped backwards so they were looking almost directly upwards as they engaged with the vision, which they described as the Blessed Mother. The young visionaries' eyes were transfixed and their bodies unresponsive to touch, including with lighted cigarettes and needle pricks. They became so heavy that strong men were unable to move them, while they could move each other (as in levitation) by just a finger or two. No sounds penetrated their ecstatic states. Some two weeks into the apparitions, the girls' behavior changed again in a remarkable way.

> *While remaining in ecstasy, the girls got to their feet and began walking with their eyes fixed on their Vision above without looking where they were going ... Then they marched, usually in tandem or threes, throughout the village, into the houses, to the church, to the cemetery, up to the Pines and back down again. They walked forward or backward and occasionally on their knees. Sometimes their forward marches were so rapid that only the young men of the village could keep up with them...and once out of ecstasy [the girls] were unaware that they had moved from one place to another.*[147]

These changes in location during ecstasy were apparently due to the apparition moving from one place to another, with the girls following. Sometimes they were seen to be moving as if on air, as Conchita's cousin, Lucia González, attested to a visiting nun, while the two women stood on the edge of the hill at the top of the Calleja. *See the de-*

cline full of rocks. Well, I saw the girls go down there back-wards without their feet touching the ground.[148] It seems that when they did fall, they were never seriously hurt. And they were unaware of the passage of time during their ecstasies. *In spite of the very difficult positions in which they held themselves, in spite of the long marches, in spite of being on their knees on top of sharp stones, their impression was al-ways that the vision had lasted only a brief time.*[149] On com-ing out of their ecstatic states, the girls would often say to visitors not to leave so soon, not realizing that the ecstasies had lasted sometimes for hours.

Another behavioral problem to cause grief for Gara-bandal critics involved reports from the children that Mary often smiled and laughed during apparitions. Heaven for-bid Jorge! During the apparition on December 8, 1961, the feast of the Immaculate Conception, Mary congratulated Conchita on her feast day (the name 'Conchita' is a con-traction of the seer's second name 'Concepción'). In a letter written just a few days after the apparition, Conchita re-ported what happened.

On the feast of the Immaculate Conception, the Blessed Virgin came and congratulated me, as indeed she told me she would come. She laughed a lot … They [the villagers] said that I went to where we had the first apparition and that I came back down to my house backwards. Then they said that I went out of the house again and recited

*the rosary in the streets, visiting all the sick and giving
them the crucifix to kiss. As you know, I am not aware of
these things. Others tell me [that I do them].*[150]

I contend that the so-called behavioral problems of
Garabandal are really reflections on the apparition—Mary's
physical location and her words and demeanor—rather
than any misconduct of the children. Ironically, the children are depicted by critics as the perpetrators of a fraud,
while Mary is the quintessential victim, unable to defend
herself. Whether she exists or not, she must remain hidden
behind the supernatural world's veil of invisibility. And if
the apparitions are not from God, runs the argument, then
they must be from the dark side.

Adverse commentary of this kind against Garabandal
seeks in effect to demonize the young seers, making them
out to be precocious false prophets and harbingers of fake
news. The facts are much less complicated, as Conchita informed John Cornwell. *I saw her [the Blessed Mother] almost every day for four years. If this turns out to be false then
nothing is true.*[151] Here is a cry from the heart, Holy Father,
from a holy woman who the Church in its mercy can release from her suffering with a proper inquiry.

I had hoped at Garabandal to explore the demonic
thing a little further. To this end, I picked up a booklet published by the Holy See, in which the opening chapter is
headed 'Pope Francis takes the devil seriously'. You speak

about sinful gossip when the devil takes control of the human heart and tongue. *The Apostle John [1 Jn 3:15] tells us that anyone who hates his brother is a murderer. We are used to gossip, to spreading rumors, and we often transform our communities as well as our families into 'hell' where this kind of crime that leads to killing one's brother and sister with one's tongue is manifest.*[152] I would go further and say that the uncontrollable anger that often drives gossip makes us all potential killers, literally, and if we think we are incapable of murdering someone then we have not met the right person.

Given my time constraints at Garabandal, perhaps I will have another opportunity to reflect on the perplexing question of evil over the next couple of days as I join my American traveling companions on a bus trip via the Camino—the Way of St James (the 'Apostle of Peace'). I expect some solitude on the pilgrim road to Santiago de Compostela, with plenty of time to think about your observations on the devil.

In the meantime, I bid you farewell from Garabandal, and I do ask for your generous and merciful consideration of the veracity of the Marian apparitions in the Cantabrian Mountains. One of the things I have in mind is the possibility you will announce a fully independent Garabandal inquiry at the same time you declare the Medjugorje apparitions 'worthy of belief as private revelation'.

Sincerely

Peter Breen

Prodigal Pilgrim Group

Pilgrim Letter 15
An Interlude on the Way of St James

Prodigal Pilgrim Group
Hotel NH Collection
Avenida do Burgo das Nacions
Santiago de Compostela, Spain

September 24, 2019
Fr Jorge Mario Bergoglio
Holy Father Pope Francis
Papal Residence
Domus Sanctae Marthae
00120 Citta del Vaticano

Dear Fr Jorge

Our Spanish tour guide was a young man named Quico
who sported braces to hold his pants up, a patchy short
beard and a broad smile whenever anybody needed help—
which was most of the time. He was deeply concerned
about climate change and the loss of biodiversity in Spain.
As the bus driver steered the tour bus to the side of the road
on the outskirts of Santiago de Compostela to allow pilgrims to 'walk' the Camino, Quico drew our attention to

the lack of bugs on the bus windscreen. Somebody blamed the devil for killing the bugs, which drew a collective groan from my corner of the bus. Nothing in the secular world raises eyebrows and rolls eyes like talk of the devil.

Soon we stood at the side of the road with our tourist backpacks and metal walking sticks, our luggage safely on its way to the hotel in the bus, which disappeared down the road in a cloud of dust. Nearby, a concrete milestone called a 'mojone', with its blue scallop shell and engraved yellow arrow to mark the Camino told me I had about ten miles to go to reach the Cathedral of St James and the pilgrims' Mass.

Within minutes we were walking in a eucalyptus forest, with the compliments of Spanish missionaries to Australia. The holy fathers had no idea that the seeds they took home were likely to grow into large forests that shed bark on the forest floor, creating fire hazards and pushing out the local varieties of beech, elm, hazelnut and oak trees.

The thought crossed my mind that missionaries would not knowingly do the work of the devil. On the other hand, I reckon that the devil was involved in the decision to log an area about the size of Pennsylvania in Canada's boreal forests for toilet paper.[153] And no less demonic, in my opinion, was the plan to extract up to 10 million gallons of water per day for the next 50 years from Australia's precious rivers and underground aquifers to establish and operate a new coalmine in North Queensland.[154] Size matters when it comes to protecting the natural environment, Holy Father, and the more destructive the project the bigger the devils involved in my correspondence.

Others will say that the work of the devil is failing to look after shareholder returns, thereby squandering investment opportunities for those of us who rely on consumption to earn our livelihoods. Many of us, in good conscience, are happy for financial security to be placed above protecting the natural environment, arguing that everything balances out in the end. You had a bit to say about insatiable and irresponsible economic growth in your encyclical on the natural environment. *We know how unsustainable the behavior of those who constantly consume and destroy, while others are not yet able to live in a way worthy of their human dignity. That is why the time has come to accept decreased growth in some parts of the world, in order to provide resources for other places to experience healthy growth.*[155]

In your booklet on the devil, you quote the Apostle Paul to explain the heart of the problem with demonic influence—we find ways to justify what we do. I do not understand my own actions, Paul says, for I do not do what I want, but the very thing I hate (Rom 7:15).[156] The devil's scales seem to be weighted against us. I try to control my sinful anger, but it's often easier to fly into a rant rather than simply to button my lip. I can easily justify the rant—often I have my say, if only to set the record straight—but it's not what I want to do. Paul confesses his sin to the community, his tendency to sin. He does not hide it.[157] And while we do not know the nature of the sin that occupied so much of Paul's attention, we do know he fought the good fight and won with the grace of God's forgiveness.

One question arises, Holy Father, about our responsibility for various forms of malfeasance that appear to be joined at the hip to a battle between good and bad angels. This battle rages long after our redemption—and even longer since the fall—a battle in which we have no say as to the armaments available to either side and the outcome of which, although known to us as the triumph of good over evil, was determined long before our meagre existence.

I think of the suffering of Conchita González and the other Garabandal visionaries, if the four years of apparitions they witnessed was just some cosmic scrap between the forces of good and evil. That would be a great injustice at the human level. Scripture tells us that the reason the Son of God appeared on Earth was to destroy the works of the devil (1 Jn 3:8), and yet the Catechism of the Catholic Church rightly concludes that it's *a great mystery that providence should [continue to] permit diabolical activity.*[158]

No less mysterious is how the sin of Adam became the sin of all his descendants. Again, the catechism is realistic if not too helpful. *By this 'unity of the human race' all men are implicated in Adam's sin, as all are implicated in Christ's justice. Still, the transmission of original sin is a mystery that we cannot fully understand.*[159] I am not sure what all that means, Holy Father—it sounds like Baptism still has some work to do. Ironically, without the stain of original sin, Christianity has no meaning. If it were not for the numerous exchanges between Jesus and Satan in Scripture—along with modern human horrors such as the Auschwitz-Birkenau death camps—the devil could quite easily be dismissed as a cautionary tale that predates human existence.

There is no simple solution to the problem of evil; but one way to cope with belief in the devil is to treat all things demonic as a matter of private opinion. For this observation about how to distance oneself from the problem of evil, I am indebted to CS Lewis and his book, *The Screwtape Letters.* You will recall the fictional correspondence in which Screwtape, the accomplished devil, instructs his pupil, Wormwood, in a series of letters on how best to encourage man away from the Light and into the Nothing. In the book's preface, Lewis explained that devils are fallen angels who abused their free will and became enemies of God (and enemies of us as a corollary), but they do not represent a power opposite to God. There can be no 'perfect badness' that stands in opposition to the perfect goodness of God. Angels and devils are opposites, in the same way that Good Man is the opposite of Bad Man. Devils are not different in nature from angels, but their nature is depraved. Satan (or Lucifer) is the leader of the devils and Michael the archangel is boss of the angels. *I believe this not in the sense that it is part of my creed, but in the sense that it is one of my opinions. My religion would not be in ruins if this opinion were shown to be false. Till that happens – and proofs of a negative are hard to come by – I shall retain it ... And it conflicts with nothing any of the sciences has shown to be true.*[160]

Angels and devils are fable or myth in the secular world, but real in the spiritual world, according to revelation about principalities and powers. For those of us who believe that Marian apparitions are real, the evidence for angels and devils is difficult to deny, since they apparently pop in and out of Mary's appearances like extras on a movie set. Mary said at Medjugorje that whenever she appeared in apparition, the devil was there too. And the visionaries at all of Mary's apparitions report angels as well as demonic disturbances. Even so, I was fascinated that Lewis was able to avoid the argument about reality and myth, by asserting belief in angels and devils as a matter of private opinion, rather than a question of faith and morals.

George Pell used to do the same thing on the question of the existence of hell. His Eminence famously told atheist Richard Dawkins on national television that although the Church teaches that a place called hell exists, it does not teach that anyone is there. Comforting as this idea may be—I have always struggled with the idea of unlimited punishment for limited human beings—the compassionate George's understanding of hell is contrary to Church tradition and other teachings as expounded in the catechism and

Scripture. But all power to George for having a private opinion contrary to Church teaching on faith and morals, and for also having the courage to express that opinion.

Which reminds me, I heard on the grapevine that you are thinking of initiating a full canonical trial into the convictions of George the convict. I caution you not to act precipitously, Holy Father. Public opinion on the cardinal's case is no less divided than the two juries and three appeal judges who have had the opportunity to consider the facts in detail.[161] A further seven High Court judges are yet to express an opinion on the convictions. The main ground for appeal to the High Court is that the trial judge and the majority judges on appeal failed to look at the big picture— the large body of evidence that contradicted the choirboy's sexual assault accusations. It may be that the lower courts have reversed the onus of proof, requiring George to prove his innocence, instead of the prosecution having to prove his guilt beyond reasonable doubt. Innocent or guilty of child sexual abuse, George has a few other things to explain. One is his opinion on climate science.

I wrote to the cardinal when he was Archbishop of Sydney, asking why his contrarian views on climate science were not heretical, given the instructions of the Vatican about the need to protect the natural environment. I ended the letter in the nicest possible way, reminding His Eminence that the Earth was never intended by God to be a rubbish tip for human consumption on an industrial scale.

George fired back a quick response. *In the Catholic Church climate change is not a matter of faith and morals and Catholics are free to come to their own views.*[162] Earlier in the same letter, George assured me I had nothing to worry about anyway, since humans had virtually nothing to do with climate change. *The other point to make is that my skepticism about claims for human activity as the cause of climate change are based on scientific evidence and that evidence suggests that the contribution of human activity [to climate change] is miniscule.*[163] For the record, I just checked the Intergovernmental Panel on Climate Change (IPCC) website and it appears that industrial and other human emissions have caused about 100 per cent of global warming observed in the last 100 years.

Poor George is forever denying that Catholics are free to come to their own views on faith and morals, and then does so himself when the need arises, as in the question of the existence of hell. He does something similar on the question of conscience, saying that the Church has never taught that the primacy of conscience was a precept of faith, but if such a precept can be found, then the Church was wrong and the teaching should be thrown out.[164] If you ever get the chance, Holy Father, you might consider speaking infallibly on the right of the faithful to hold private opinions—even if those opinions seem to be contrary to Church teaching on faith and morals.

To sum up, I have some sympathy for the cardinal's predicament in prison for crimes he may not have committed, but there is such a thing as utilitarian punishment—as I mentioned in a previous letter. Many people have suffered horrendous crimes at the hands of the clergy and have never experienced justice for those crimes. Who would deny them the opportunity to feel vindicated by Pell's convictions? If the cardinal is innocent, then he will never have a better chance of moving mountains in the spiritual world than through his unjust suffering in prison. If he is guilty, then his repeated denials of the crimes will be consuming his soul. Either way, I wonder if he still thinks nobody goes to hell?[165]

After about an hour on the Camino, skirting around the devils in my head and the stones at my feet, I came across a commotion to the side of the path near an open field. A woman from our group had either lost her footing and fallen to the ground, or was just sitting there, exhausted. She was surrounded by comforters, including our priest leader, Fr Ben. I should say, Holy Father, that there was little concern on the Camino for interlopers like us—day trippers walking just the last few miles—when the serious walkers had been on the road for more than a week. I joined the Good Samaritans to help the pilgrim, although one of the devils in me wanted to join the biblical priest and the Levite who kept walking. Together we coaxed the woman back to her feet and shuffled along for another mile or so, but it came as no surprise to see our tour bus at the next road-house, with our driver waiting patiently.

We arrived in Santiago de Compostela by bus in time for the midday Pilgrims Mass, only to learn that the Cathedral of St James was closed for renovations, and the Mass would be held in the nearby Church of St Francis of Assisi. As you know, your namesake made a pilgrimage from Italy more than 800 years ago, and founded the church that bears his name. The present Baroque-style church built in about 1750 was packed to the rafters for a Mass celebrated in several languages, to acknowledge pilgrims from different countries.

After Mass, I stood in the paved courtyard at the front of the church, beside a granite monolith some 30 feet high, dominated by the iconic Cross of St Francis. In the courtyard I met a tall young man from California who had walked with a Spanish group for nearly 500 miles, from the Basilica of Our Lady of the Pillar in Saragossa—the place where tradition holds that Mary first appeared on Earth to the Apostle James (the patron saint of pilgrims) in the year 40 CE. The young man's destination, he proudly informed me, was Apparition Hill in Medjugorje—the place of Mary's final earthly apparitions. He asked what I hoped to gain from my pilgrimage; I heard myself nominate an insight into sinful anger as a good outcome for the journey.

I was leaving my American friends the next day for a flight to Dubrovnik via Rome, to be followed by a two-hour trip by bus or taxi to Medjugorje. Perhaps the young man and I were on the same flight from Santiago airport? He was taking a different route, he told me, but we might catch up in Medjugorje's Church of St James, where pilgrims from all over the world make their peace with God.

Sincerely
Peter Breen
Prodigal Pilgrim Group

Part Four

The Signs of Medjugorje
1981-2021

Pilgrim Letter 16

A Perfume of Roses in Full Bloom

Prodigal Pilgrim Group
Hotel Sulic
Vukovarska 13, Medjugorje
Bosnia & Herzegovina

October 1, 2019

Fr Jorge Mario Bergoglio
Holy Father Pope Francis
Papal Residence
Domus Sanctae Marthae
00120 Citta del Vaticano

Dear Fr Jorge

I finally made it to my destination—the last place of Marian apparitions on Earth. Back in 1991, when I first travelled to Medjugorje, it was a rural village roughly laid out in a triangle formed by St James Church, Podbrdo (Apparition Hill) and Mount Krizevac (Cross Mountain). The cross was built in 1933, to mark 1,900 years since the death of Jesus of Nazareth. Local villagers built the cross after carrying steel, sand, and bags of concrete up a narrow limestone and dirt track to the top of the mountain, which rises a thousand feet above the village. Today the triangle is showing signs of both wear and prosperity—Medjugorje is the fastest growing place of pilgrimage in the world. You can walk the triangle in half a day, Holy Father, or allow a full day if you include the 14 Stations of the Cross that lead to the 16-ton cross on Krizevac.

Podbrdo is a much more forgiving climb than Krizevac. On my first pilgrimage to Medjugorje nearly 30 years ago, I was rewarded near the top of the hill with the mystical smell of roses in full bloom. Some in the group I traveled with at the time experienced gold dust falling onto the rocky path at their feet, while others insisted the sun was spinning and throwing off all the colors of the rainbow. I could not vouch for the gold dust or the spinning sun, but the roses were an unexpected treat. When it happened, I was unaware that a strong scent of roses was a feature of Marian apparition shrines, going back to Our Lady of Guadalupe on the outskirts of Mexico City in 1531.

Podbrdo or Apparition Hill is the place where Mary first appeared (some people say 'allegedly') to two teenage girls on June 24, 1981. Four more children witnessed the apparition the following day. And all six visionaries have continued to experience the phenomenon for the nearly 40 years since it began. The six are Mirjana Soldo, Marija Pavlovic-Lunetti, Ivanka Ivankovic, Jakov Colo, Vicka Mijatovic and Ivan Dragicevic. Three of the visionaries have received nine of ten secrets from Mary about future events on Earth and still witness the apparition daily. The other three have received all ten secrets and are visited occasionally— either once each year and/or monthly. All the 'children' are now aged in their late forties or early fifties. They are all married with children and still spend most of their time in the village.

St James Church in Medjugorje, built and consecrated as recently as 1969, is dedicated to the Apostle of Peace and patron saint of pilgrims. Like the Cathedral of St James in Santiago de Compostela (consecrated in 1211), St James Church in Medjugorje welcomes pilgrims from all over the world, of all faiths and no faith. Prodigal pilgrims who wander in and out of their faith are especially welcome.

The Medjugorje church has become the second-most photographed church in the world—second only to St Peter's in Rome—according to a French website dedicated to Medjugorje statistics. I apologize, Holy Father, for quoting such a dodgy statistic (who could possibly be keeping the count?) but a picture is worth a thousand words as the cliché goes, and my enthusiasm for Medjugorje is not above cliché. All that said, the possibility still exists that Medjugorje is the biggest fraud or the longest mass hysteria event in human history, although the weight of evidence is heavily against both of those propositions in my correspondence.

On my first trip, I recall going through the medical and scientific evidence for the apparitions in amazement. As at

Garabandal, the children were wired up to all sorts of contraptions to measure what was happening in their brains and to their eyes and ears during ecstasy. They were pinched, burnt, needle-pricked, pushed and pulled while gazing wide-eyed at the apparition, and no reactions were recorded on the machines monitoring their minds or bodies. The focal lengths of their eyes suggested they were looking at an object some two meters away. Loud noises—including a gunshot—caused no response in their brain wave patterns. *Other instruments checked the normality of heartbeat, sight, hearing and voice production. Light flashed in their eyes by an electro-oculogram during ecstasy caused no blinking or other reaction.*[166]

Renowned medical teams from Milan and Paris examined the children during their apparitions, using the latest scientific equipment, and *independently validated the legitimacy of their state of ecstasy as being in some form of true communication outside their ordinary time-space experience. These scientific studies also ruled out any possibility of 'collective hallucination' and, by deduction, any form of mere human deception or falsification.*[167] Perhaps the most remarkable feature of the apparitions over nearly 40 years is the complete absence of conflict between the visionaries, as to what they were seeing or the information being conveyed to them.

From July 4, 1981, the children witnessed the apparition wherever they happened to be at around twenty to six in the evening. At the appointed time, they went into ecstasy separately or as a group, regardless of their location—the phenomenon known as bilocation. Mary appeared to the visionaries simultaneously, whether they were in different parts of a building, different parts of the village, on opposite sides of the country or even when they were traveling in separate aircraft. The apparition had no regard for time differences: if the visionaries happened to be in different countries, Mary appeared to them at twenty to six Medjugorje time—irrespective of local times.

Wherever she appeared to the Medjugorje visionaries, Mary arrived in a globe of light as at Lourdes, Fatima and Garabandal, and others, apart from the six visionaries often witnessed the light. Others also witnessed the synchronicity of the visionaries during ecstasy, when Mary appeared to them as a group. They moved from their normal state into ecstasy in perfect unison, they knelt or stood as one and they prayed together as if with one voice. When the apparition departed, the children came out of ecstasy at the same moment. *All this is regarded as proof at least of objectivity since there is clearly no collusion or prearranged signal. Can one assume that they are seeing and communicating with an object or person science cannot identify?*[168]

As the children became more at ease with the idea of a supernatural visitor, they asked Mary about the signs and wonders the people were seeing. The children reported Mary answering their questions by saying that God gives the grace to witness the phenomena. *My children, have you not observed that the faith began to extinguish itself? ... [the signs are] necessary to awaken the faith ... [they are] a gift from God.*[169]

The faith of the local firefighters was put to the test on October 28, 1981, when they were called to extinguish a fire on Apparition Hill, at the very place where the children first witnessed the apparition four months earlier. *Several hundred people stood and watched this conspicuous blaze for fifteen minutes until police and firemen arrived to deal with it: but no bonfire, no brazier, no embers, no ash nor any other trace of fire could be found. That evening Gospa [the name for 'Our Lady' in Croatian] told the children that the fire was a small herald of the great sign that was to come.*[170]

You will recall from an earlier letter, Holy Father, my guess that the visible and permanent sign to be left on Apparition Hill at the end of the apparitions could be a modern version of Moses' burning bush. Well, you will not be surprised to learn that my speculation arose from this incident with the puzzled firemen and Mary's later observations about the great sign. Nothing turns on my speculation, of course, and I could be way off the mark. Fire and light are both popular with pundits and I see no reason why the sign could not include both elements.

When the events associated with the ten secrets come to pass, the world as we know it will be changed forever, according to the visionaries. These secrets are regarded as an important part of Mary's messages and are said *to concern the future of this planet, and when all the children know all the secrets the visions will cease.*[171] The three visionaries who have received all ten secrets are Mirjana Soldo, Ivanka Ivankovic and Jakov Colo. Each secret is a prophecy of a future event and Mirjana bears the responsibility of revealing the secrets three days before each event takes place.

The first three secrets are said to be warnings which will draw the world's attention to Medjugorje. Mirjana said of the first warning: *If the people saw the first secret, as it was shown to me, all of them would most certainly be shaken enough to take a new and different look at themselves and everything around them.*[172] In her extraordinary book on Medjugorje, Mirjana reported Mary using powerful language: *I implore you to stop for a moment and to reflect on yourselves and on the transience of this your earthly life.*[173]

As for the second warning or secret, commentators seem to agree that it's the same future event as Garabandal's prophesied sign in the sky *visible in every part of the world* according to Conchita González—a flash of light like two stars colliding. It will be followed by the 'Illumination of the Soul' if the late Wayne Weible is to be believed,[174] based on his assessment of the writings of a long line of Christian mystics and prophets including the children at Garabandal.

The third warning or secret will likely be the same event as Garabandal's Great Miracle followed by the visible and permanent sign, which Wayne Weible described as *something that has never before been seen on earth.*[175] In an interview with writer Mario Vasilj published in 2015, Mirjana confirmed that the Medjugorje sign will self-evidently not be of this world. She would not call the sign a secret, but *a gift to Medjugorje and the entire world, so that everyone can see that Our Lord sent the Holy Mother to us and she was here among us.*[176] Mirjana also reported Mary saying that the sign will be given for the benefit of unbelievers whom she loves as much as believers. *She loves you and all her children as much as she loves me.*[177]

We know nothing about the fourth, fifth and sixth secrets of Medjugorje, except that they might involve local issues in the village or personal matters related to the visionaries. We do know that the seventh secret is a chastisement, the impact of which has been diminished by the prayers, reconciliations and conversions achieved through the supplications of the visionaries and their supporters. Mirjana was shocked when she received the seventh secret, and she asked Mary if anything could be done to ease it. When Mary told her to pray, Mirjana raised a veritable prayer army of priests, nuns, and friends to implore God to alleviate the suffering of the seventh secret.

Mirjana was surprised by what happened next. *A couple of months after that, Our Lady told me that the seventh secret had really been eased and that I should never again ask her about the secrets, because they were God's will which may not be changed.*[178] Well, it seems that God's will may not be changed, except when Mary intervenes on our behalf.

A courageous and almost defiant Mirjana Soldo was shocked again when she received the eighth secret—another chastisement—and she prayed intensely to Mary to intercede for God's mercy. Mary responded by saying *I have prayed; the punishment has been softened. Repeated prayers and fasting reduce punishments from God, but it is not possible to avoid entirely the chastisement. Go on the streets of the city, count those who glorify God and those who offend Him. God can no longer endure that.*[179] It follows that praying through Mary for the impact of a specific chastisement to be diminished is not futile, even if it's no surprise that we have already incurred God's wrath.

As to the ninth secret, all we know is to expect another severe chastisement which may be diminished by prayer and fasting, but it will not be eliminated.

The tenth secret is said to be the most severe of all the Medjugorje chastisements. According to the visionaries who know the tenth secret, it will be a purification of the world and therefore is a matter of grave concern. But otherwise, they have said nothing about the event. Whether Medjugorje's tenth secret is the same event as Garabandal's Great Chastisement nobody seems to know. The young visionaries at Garabandal said the Great Chastisement will be the fulfillment of the prophecies from the Nights of Screams.

Author and publisher Barry Hanratty, an expert on Garabandal, said the Great Chastisement is generally accepted to be the same event as the 'Three Days of Darkness' prophesied by Blessed Anna-Maria Taigi, but Barry gave no authority for this proposition.[180] Wayne Weible made a similar connection between the tenth secret of Medjugorje and three days of darkness. In his book about Mary's last apparition, Wayne listed more than ten Church mystics and saints, including Padre Pio, who prophesied three days of darkness. Wayne said that the multiplicity of prophecies gives credibility to the event. *So many confirming prophecies lend the air of truth to belief that it will occur.*[181] Yes, but not necessarily in the context of Mary's modern apparitions. None of the visionaries at Garabandal or Medjugorje has said anything publicly about three days of darkness.

Dare I say, it's not my place to cavil with a long list of mystics and saints, but simply to point out that we do not know what the tenth secret of Medjugorje will look like. It may involve three days of darkness, or that might be something else not to look forward to further down the track. One of many things I agree with Wayne Weible about is the prospect of God being more actively and obviously present in human affairs after the Medjugorje secrets are revealed.[182] For the moment, Holy Father, you may be interested in my personal encounter with three days of metaphorical darkness in Medjugorje, an experience worthy of a separate letter.

Sincerely

Peter Breen

Prodigal Pilgrim Group

Pilgrim Letter 17

Three Days of Darkness in Medjugorje

Prodigal Pilgrim Group
Hotel Sulic
Vukovarska 13, Medjugorje
Bosnia & Herzegovina

October 8, 2019

Fr Jorge Mario Bergoglio
Holy Father Pope Francis
Papal Residence
Domus Sanctae Marthae
00120 Citta del Vaticano

Dear Fr Jorge

Medjugorje today is a bit of a shock for those of us who first visited the shrine in 1991, especially the proliferation of shops, hotels, and apartment buildings. Many apartments are owned by foreigners, who leave their investments locked up for the future. No judgment on my part, Holy Father, just a passing observation that too much money is no less problematic than too little for those of us who seek to serve God.

In 1991, I wanted to stay in Medjugorje and help spread the messages of conversion, reconciliation, and peace through my mystery novel about the third secret of Fatima. Instead, I watched in horror at my diminishing bank balance when I was unable to find a publisher. I went home chastened and poor—though only by the standards of first world countries. Ever since, I have wondered whether I was like the rich young man who went away sad when Jesus asked him to sell his worldly possessions and give the money to the poor (Mt 19:16-30).

I could hardly believe I was back in Medjugorje with another book about basically the same Marian prophecy. I wondered if I was one more biblical eleventh-hour worker in the vineyard or just another writer on a frolic of his own? Would I still be willing to give up everything to help spread the Medjugorje messages? My wife reminds me of an old Buddhist proverb: the lessons become more gross, the longer it takes to learn them. Did the rich young man who went away sad become old and bitter? Perhaps he lost all his wealth anyway, and morphed into the Prodigal Son of Scripture? Or did he do as I did and went away and partied, only to find himself unable to comprehend the mess he had made or what he might do to help clean it up?

What strikes me most about Medjugorje today is the sense of 'koompartoo'—an Australian Aboriginal word meaning new beginning or fresh start. After morning Mass on the second day of my pilgrimage, I walked down the tree-lined avenue called Via Domini that runs from the outside altar at the back of St James Church to the cemetery. Walking past the mosaic depictions of the mysteries of the rosary, I was reminded of my last crisis of faith in 1990, when I tried to recall the mysteries of the rosary at Fatima. Then there were just fifteen mysteries. Of course, your predecessor, Pope John Paul II, has added the five mysteries of light, which I now find difficult to recall.

Just beyond the mosaics, I stumbled across a 30-feet high bronze statue, which I had read about but never seen in the metal. Known as the 'Risen Christ' by Slovenian sculptor Andrija Ajdic, the statue is a modern representation of Jesus on the cross, 'risen up' as in lifted up from a bronze imprint of the cross on the ground. Two lines of pilgrims queued for 30 yards to pay homage to the statue. As a work of art, the installation is exquisite; but the queuing pilgrims were more interested in a tear-like substance that is said to leak from the right knee of the statue. Most pilgrims in the queue carried tissues or soft cloths, sold in the religious artefact shops for the purpose of wiping the knee. Claims abound that the 'tears' have healing qualities. All I could think of was the Israelites worshipping a golden calf as they waited for Moses to return from Mt Sinai with the Ten Commandments. No surprise that the first of God's commandments prohibited idolatry.

That evening, I met my new pilgrim companions for the first time—another group of Americans who had arrived that day from New York—and I complained mercilessly to them about the leaky knee Jesus. To a man and a woman, they were patient if unsympathetic. The group's spiritual director, a secular priest from Washington, told me that the Church exercises discretion in the matter of private revelation and we have no business questioning the faith of others. Besides, the 'tears' have been tested and found to be 99 per cent water, so they are quite likely the result of condensation formed by moist air on the cold metal of the statue. Somebody else volunteered that the bronze statue is mostly hollow and microscopic holes in the metal allow moisture to escape from inside the installation. Later that evening, I called Australia and spoke to my wife, Diane, who reminded me that God meets people in different places.

Early the next day, when the air was cold and morning dew could be expected to form on metal surfaces, I made my way to the 'Risen Christ' statue and stood at the end of the shortest of the two queues. I was reminded of the 'holy dip' queue at Lourdes, and it occurred to me that even if the 'tears' were ordinary water, that was no reason to exclude the possibility that they may have healing properties through God's grace. I looked up and down the queue for someone to annoy with my questions, but heads were bowed in reverence or buried in neck scarves to keep out the cold air. Most people carried rosary beads and I watched supple fingers slip silently from one bead to the next, as we all shuffled along at a snail's pace.

Twenty minutes later, I mounted the two wooden steps that allowed me to look directly at the highly polished metal knee, and the first thing I can report is that it was as dry as a bone. For the sake of the exercise, I rubbed furiously with a paper tissue, and I tapped and patted the structure with my fingers. It sounded hollow, but as you might expect, there were no microscopic holes I could bear witness to.

To my mind, the crying knee scandalized the artist's work, a masterpiece that merged Jesus' death and resurrection. How could an art installation that gave glory to God be compromised by idolatry, masquerading as piety and devotion? After complaining to my wife and fellow pilgrims and railing against God for allowing such a scandal, the thought occurred to me that perhaps I was the idolater. What was more important: a metal artwork or a person's faith and trust in God? I tried praying about the problem to no avail. Unfinished prayers rattled around inside my head. Reciting the rosary put me to sleep.

For three days, I tried to ignore the 'Risen Christ' statue, until finally, late in the afternoon of the third day, I sat on one of the wooden benches that face the installation, fanning out like an amphitheater. Almost in disbelief, I watched as pilgrims continued to climb the two wooden steps to rub, wipe or kiss the metal knee. Soon enough, I reached a stalemate with myself. One voice in my head kept saying *How can anyone believe that stuff.* Another emanating from my heart insisted that *God meets people in differ-*

ent places. Exasperated to the point of mental exhaustion, I thumbed through various pamphlets and papers I had picked up from local bookshops.

I found myself reading Mary's message to Marija Pavlovic-Lunetti of the previous month in which the Mother of Jesus urged us to pray the rosary and meditate on the mysteries of the rosary *because, in your life, you are also passing through joys and sorrows.* Mary said that placing our lives in God's hands through the mysteries of the rosary is transformative. *In this way, you will have the experience of faith like Peter [the Apostle], who met Jesus, and the Holy Spirit filled his heart.*[183] Another pamphlet reminded me that the Apostle Paul said we cannot believe in Jesus except through his Spirit—nobody can say 'Jesus is Lord' except by the grace of the Holy Spirit (1 Cor 12:3).

What we hope and pray for is that the Spirit of God will actively dispense divine grace to good people of all faiths and no faith, especially those with an open mind about the existence of God. From the early days of Medjugorje, Mary insisted that all people are equal before God even if some of their religious beliefs are off the beaten track. *She loves the atheist as much as she loves the believer* according to Mirjana Soldo,[184] whose mission it is to reach out to unbelievers.

I hope you are still reading, Holy Father, since there is one more aspect of faith I wanted to raise with you. As you know, the Catholic Catechism says that true believers will have certainty, as well as the requisite divine grace and human will. When I was a child, the community was sharply divided between 'Catholics' and 'Publics', which roughly reflected the post-war public and private school education systems. A popular joke of the day asked why parts of heaven were walled off; the answer was that Catholics were behind the wall, because they believed they were the only ones who were there.

The sentiment persists in some Catholic circles, aided and abetted by the idea that God's inability to lie somehow elides into the certainty of our faith. Well, it should be said that our certainty is no different from the certainty of a devout Hindu, Buddhist, Muslim or Jew, or the growing number of devout Christian believers who are quite certain they do not want their faith and morals bolted together for the purpose of defining papal infallibility. I tell anyone who asks that you are about as interested in acting infallibly as the man in the moon—although that is a presumption on my part. But as the pope who says *the least serious sins are the sins of the flesh*,[185] you are also more likely to be a faith and ethics man rather than a faith and morals one. Please forgive me if I am misquoting you, Holy Father, or making incorrect assumptions. Better still, write and alert me to my errors, so that I may correct the record. I have enough misdeeds to confess without adding to the list the sin of calumny, which I know you detest.

Speaking of sin and confession, the sacrament of reconciliation is hugely popular at Medjugorje, with queues outside confessional boxes in the church grounds rivaling the 'Risen Christ' statue queues. I joined one of the reconciliation queues, after giving up on my dilemma at the art installation. Since you have never been to Medjugorje, you may not have experienced confession the way the priests organize it in the village. Each priest is on display, sitting in his confessional box with the languages he speaks in bold letters above the lintel over the doorway. There is no confessional door, no privacy and no pressure, even though the priest faces the penitent at his feet on a wooden kneeler as well as those in the queue waiting to confess. Priests who miss out on a confessional box sit quietly on wooden benches reading their breviaries. I reckon Medjugorje priests—locals and visitors alike—receive special graces of patience and insight during confessions. Medjugorje is described as *the confessional of the world.*[186]

One of the priests sitting on the wooden benches in his black soutane and white clerical collar looked vaguely familiar. On the ground at his feet were his backpack and a flat sign that read 'English'. As he looked up from his breviary, the priest caught me staring at him. With a wave of his hand, he summoned me to join him on the wooden bench. When the lights went on, I realized he was the tall young man who walked from Saragossa to Santiago de Compostela. As I sat beside him on the wooden bench, he offered to hear my confession. I asked for a moment to collect my thoughts and to recover from the shock that the pilgrim I had met at the foot of the St Francis Cross was also a priest.

I confessed my usual array of sins (mostly thought crimes these days) and the priest asked how I was going with my sinful anger. The question caught me off guard and what followed was a confronting interrogation by the priest. We agreed I had no desire for feelings of power or manipulation of others; we agreed I had no pressing need to be in control; we ruled out anger directed at injustice, which we agreed would not normally be sinful. That left anger aimed at myself—in the same vein as self-harm— which the priest said was often caused by one or more of the three Ds: disappointment, despair, and disillusionment. When that idea sank in, it caught the back of my throat. I had nothing more to volunteer and the priest asked no more questions.

He said a short prayer over me, praying that I might re- ceive the grace of the Holy Spirit. I remembered Emil Milat's advice that we need God's grace to learn how to separate ourselves from our egos and surrender to God. For my penance, the priest suggested I pray one decade of the rosary. Then he recited the words of absolution, which have their own magic.

God the Father of mercies, through the death and resur- rection of his Son has reconciled the world to himself and sent the Holy Spirit among us for the forgiveness of sins;

*through the ministry of the Church may God give you
pardon and peace, and I absolve you from your sins in
the name of the Father, and of the Son and of the Holy
Spirit. Amen.* [187]

I thanked the priest and headed back down the Via
Domini towards the 'Risen Christ' statue. It was almost
dark, but in the distance I could still see the two undimin-
ished queues of pilgrims waiting to climb the two wooden
steps to reach the crying knee. On arriving at one of the
benches in front of the bronze statue, I sat down to gaze at
the emerging stars. After about an hour of watching the
night sky and glimpsing the slow procession of pilgrims
kissing and stroking the shiny knee, I was finally aware of
tears—my own. All devout believers reflect God's love, and
by their lives, give witness to their faith. [188]

For a moment, I imagined I could see the word MIR
('PEACE' in Croatian) amongst the stars, but surely it was a
memory from reports I had read of the early days of the apparitions, when the word sometimes appeared in the evening sky over Mount Krizevac. It dawned on me at the 'Risen
Christ' statue that peace is impossible when we have one
story in our head and an opposing story in our heart. How
can I feel compassion and love in my heart for devout people paying homage to God and at the same time have a story in my head that calls into question their belief? Whatever
the triumph of Mary's heart might be, Holy Father, I pray

that it includes a peaceful alignment of hearts and minds about the existence of God and the nature of worship.

Sincerely
Peter Breen
Prodigal Pilgrim Group

Pilgrim Letter 18

Six Visionaries on the Same Prophetic Page

Prodigal Pilgrim Group

Hotel Sulic

Vukovarska 13, Medjugorje

Bosnia & Herzegovina

October 17, 2019

Fr Jorge Mario Bergoglio

Holy Father Pope Francis

Papal Residence

Domus Sanctae Marthae

00120 Citta del Vaticano

Dear Fr Jorge

Of all the Medjugorje magic I have seen over the years, nothing is quite as alluring to me as the document Mary handed to Mirjana Soldo on December 25, 1982, when the young visionary received her last daily apparition and the last of the ten secrets. She knelt beside her mother, father, and brother during this apparition. The family bears witness to Mirjana receiving the document—a rolled-up scroll or parchment—in her outstretched hand as if out of thin air. Mirjana said later that Mary held out the scroll, *explaining that all ten secrets were written on it … I took it from her hand without looking at it.*[189] Distressed and distracted following the apparition, at the prospect of no longer seeing the vision each day, Mirjana suddenly realized that she was still holding the scroll she had been given. How could it happen that Mary left something behind that apparently had its origin in another world? The fact of the document is mind-boggling and yet Mirjana is quite relaxed about it.

> *Having always seen Our Lady as a physical being, it seemed natural at that time to take the object from her hand, just as I would from anyone. But [when] the apparition was over, I was awestruck to see the scroll still with me … Beige in color, the scroll was made of a material akin to parchment – not quite paper and not quite fabric. I carefully unrolled it and found all ten secrets written in a simple and elegant cursive handwriting … The secrets were not numbered, but they appeared in order, one after another, with the first secret at the top and the tenth at the bottom, and they included the dates of the future events.*[190]

For a long time, Mirjana worried about the security of the words on the parchment, until she discovered that other people were unable to read them. She said Mary instructed her to give the scroll to a priest of her choosing, ten days before each of the predicted events. The priest would be able to read the words of the secret at that time, although the words of the remaining secrets would remain obscure. Three days before each event, Mirjana and the priest were to reveal the secret. Mirjana has chosen Fr Petar Ljubicic, a Franciscan priest posted to the nearby village of Tihaljina at the time of the first apparition in 1981, to help reveal the secrets. Recently he was assigned as chaplain to the parish of Vitina near Medjugorje.

Fr Petar speaks with humility about his role in revealing the secrets and he is happy to pass on the limited information at his disposal. He confirms that the first three secrets will draw attention to Medjugorje and that the third secret is the promised sign which the visionaries say is primarily intended for those who do not know God. *At the same time, the sign will be a call to all people to change their lives and turn to God ... Therefore, we should be awaiting revelation of the secrets as comfort, support and joy and not as something apocalyptic.*[191]

Fr Petar was asked whether the 'Official Church' would change its opinion about Medjugorje when the secrets are revealed.

There are many trustworthy proofs speaking in favor of the authenticity of the Medjugorje apparitions. For example, it takes two cases of miraculous healings to proclaim a saint was a person who was living a virtuous and pious life. Medjugorje has witnessed so many miraculous healings and true conversions that it could be immediately proclaimed a place of supernatural happenings. However, that has not happened yet. Revelation of the secrets will play a decisive role in the Church's coming to recognize the apparitions.[192]

At the risk of repeating myself, Holy Father, the 'Official Church' did not wait for the secrets of Fatima to be revealed, before approving the apparitions at the Cova da Iria as 'worthy of belief'. Waiting for the secrets of Medjugorje before converting (read 'believing') is doing exactly what the Blessed Mother urges us not to do. Now is the time for conversion and reconciliation—the time when God's grace is available in abundance. *At this moment, according to Our Lady, we are living in a time of grace. After this will come the time of the secrets, and the time of her triumph.*[193]

Why does the Church not want to be in the vanguard of the era of peace? After all, the Church is in the business of warning us about the future, whether of heaven, hell or global warming. Mary asks us to renew the church and build a bridge to the new world with our priests.[194] As our pope, you chose the name of St Francis who was tasked with rebuilding the Church, so approving Medjugorje would simply be carrying out your mission. Jumping on the bandwagon after the prophesied secrets are revealed will not be such a good look.

I have heard all the objections to the veracity of the apparitions and they are mere candles to the sun alongside the testimony of the six visionaries—on track and on message for four decades. From the very beginning, they have been on the same prophetic page. Nothing they said causes concern in Scripture, Church teaching or tradition, and I cannot recall one disagreement or contradiction between them.

When Ivanka received the tenth secret on May 7, 1985, Mary told her that *the grace which you and the others received, nobody on this Earth has received up until now.*[195] Mary also told the six visionaries that Medjugorje would be the fulfillment of Fatima. Consider the enthusiastic support of your predecessor, Pope John Paul II, who you canonized on April 27, 2014. Has a more devoted servant of Our Lady of Fatima occupied the seat of St Peter? Artistic depictions and secondary relics of the saintly pope are to be found in almost every corner of the Fatima shrine. He invited Mirjana to Castel Gandolfo and told her to look after Medjugorje—*the hope for the entire world.*[196] And Pope John Paul II was not inclined to limit his support for the Medjugorje apparitions to the first seven appearances, as the Vatican commission of inquiry (the Ruini report) set up by your immediate predecessor, Pope Benedict XVI, seemed inclined to do.

It makes no sense that Mary would appear at Medjugorje for seven days in June 1981, and then for the next 40 years the young visionaries would somehow mimic and ex-

pand upon those appearances to perpetrate a fraud. I would
be sending that Vatican commission back to the drawing
board, Holy Father, to find out what's happening on the
ground. You have spoken about the importance of considering what the Holy Spirit is saying to the laity—the 'sensus
fidelium'.[197]

Another thing to consider is the exemplary characters
of all six visionaries who have devoted their lives to spreading the Medjugorje messages of peace, prayer, reconciliation, fasting and conversion. They are all happily married
with children, working tirelessly with the pilgrims, and
growing in grace and wisdom. You cannot live like that if
you are living a lie in my experience. Judge them by their
fruits, Holy Father. Vicka, Ivanka, Mirjana and Jakov live in
the village with their families. Ivan and his American family
spend half the year in the USA and the other half in Medjugorje, while Marija married an Italian and they divide their
time between Italy and Medjugorje. Ivan, Marija and Vicka
are yet to receive the tenth secret. They continue to bear
witness each day to the apparition wherever they happen to
be at twenty to six in the evening.

Ivanka and Mirjana were the first of the children to see
Mary on June 24, 1981, when they were walking in the vicinity of Podbrdo Hill. As they looked up the hill about a
hundred yards away, they could clearly see the figure of a
lady wearing a bluish-grey dress. Ivan and Vicka momentarily joined Ivanka and Mirjana, before all four children

ran away terrified. Returning the next day with Marija and Jakov, the now six children found that news of the apparition had spread, and half the village was waiting at Podbrdo to see what all the fuss was about. As soon as 'the Lady' appeared—further up the hill than the previous day—the six children raced towards her for a closer look.

The onlookers below were baffled as they watched us scale the steep slope at an impossible speed, seemingly coasting over boulders and thorn bushes. Some people tried to run after us, but they could not keep pace. I was a city girl and not particularly athletic, but it felt effortless. It was as if I simply glided – or like something carried me – to the place where the woman was standing ... The first time I gazed upon the woman up close, I realized she was not of this world. Immediately and involuntarily, we fell to our knees. Not sure what to say or do, we began to pray ... To our astonishment, the woman prayed along with us.[198]

Mirjana lived with her parents in an apartment at Sarajevo in 1981, but visited Medjugorje during summer holidays, staying with her aunt, uncle, and cousins in the village. Ten years after the apparitions began, Mirjana and her family were obliged to abandon the Sarajevo apartment, when the city came under attack during the Bosnian War and the apartment building was bombed. Mirjana went to Italy with her husband Marko and their daughter Veronika.

On returning to Medjugorje after the war, Mirjana asked a United Nations peace-keeping soldier, who was travelling to Sarajevo, to see if he could find any papers in the family's abandoned apartment. A few months later, the soldier returned to Medjugorje and handed Mirjana a package containing the paperwork he had found. Among the papers was the parchment Mary had given to Mirjana during the last of her daily apparitions on December 25, 1982.

The magic of the Medjugorje parchment is comparable to the Lourdes healing spring and the Fatima spinning sun. All include Mary's prophecies in advance of the phenomena. Of course, the elephant in the room at Lourdes and Fatima is that the young seers, Bernadette Soubirous and Lucia dos Santos, both became nuns, giving a level of control to the Church over those prophetic voices. Such a constraint is unimaginable at Medjugorje, where the visionaries speak not with one voice but six. I wonder if Medjugorje might now be approved by the Church if the visionaries had decided to become nuns and priests instead of mums and dads?

On the upside, Holy Father, Mary has been free to instruct the Medjugorje visionaries about the era of peace in the context of the family and the journey of faith lived in the secular world. On the downside, some conflict has arisen between what Mary has had to say to the visionaries and traditional Church teaching. Not that the conflict is serious—more in the nature of new information about the next life, which the Church is unable to verify. For example, the private revelation from Medjugorje that we go straight from this life to the next and immediately receive a new transfigured body, is one idea that has put a cat amongst a few theological pigeons, who look forward to the resurrection of a corporeal blood and bone body.

Personally, I am inclined to believe that Mary knows more about the next life than the best of theologians. A more important question is whose plan to change the world are we following: God's plan or Mary's? This question arose when two of my traveling companions insisted Mary had a plan to change the world, while I had the temerity to suggest they were putting the cart before the horse.

If Mary has a plan to change the world, it can only be one revealed by God, and numerous statements supporting that proposition are recorded in interviews with the visionaries. Two examples from Mirjana's book illustrate the point. The visionary wrote about the possibility that you, Holy Father, might one day be so bold as to find the Medjugorje apparitions 'worthy of belief'. *But I never worry about Vatican approval because I know what I see. I trust in God's plan, and I've put everything in Our Lady's hands. I simply focus on my mission.*[199] In another part of the book, Mirjana was unambiguous about working to advance God's plan. *Some people wonder why there are secrets at all, but it was not Our Lady who decided to have it this way. Everything will happen according to God's will.* [200]

Assuming God has a plan to change the world, Holy Father, the next question is what does that plan look like?

Sincerely

Peter Breen

Prodigal Pilgrim Group

Pilgrim Letter 19
A Theory of God's Plan to Change the World

Prodigal Pilgrim Group

Hotel Sulic

Vukovarska 13, Medjugorje

Bosnia & Herzegovina

October 27, 2019

Fr Jorge Mario Bergoglio

Holy Father Pope Francis

Papal Residence

Domus Sanctae Marthae

00120 Citta del Vaticano

Dear Fr Jorge

Forgive me for putting forward a theory about God becoming more openly involved in human affairs, but the direction in which we are traveling seems to me to demand divine attention, if we hope to avoid going to environmental hell.

On the face of it, the world looks quite splendid from where I sit in my comfortable first-class window seat, enjoying the cabin service and the view from spaceship Earth, as it hurtles through time and space at 67,000 miles per hour on a journey around the Sun. My time on board is a nanosecond in the human odyssey when measured against home base in the Milky Way Galaxy (traveling at 448,000 miles per hour), which is expected to collide with its nearest neighbor, the Andromeda Galaxy, in about four billion years. The God plan I am familiar with tells me we will still be around in some form at that time, perhaps enjoying platinum cabin service and even more spectacular views from spaceship Heaven.

But spaceship Earth will remain the mothership for as long as it exists, and therein lies the problem. Passengers are killing off the life support systems that power spaceship Earth, threatening to make the planet indistinguishable in the galaxy from spaceship Mars. Apart from destroying the natural environment, some seriously rich though truly demented first-class passengers are spending their wealth trying to jump ship to spaceship Mars, when they could be funding programs to restore the Earth's life support systems. You could hardly blame God for wanting to change the world.

Meanwhile, war has erupted between first-class and coach-class passengers as to who bears the primary responsibility for destroying spaceship Earth's life support systems. Of the 7.7 billion passengers currently on board, about half live in poverty (less than $5.50 per day), while the gap between rich and poor grows exponentially. The richest eight first-class passengers now control half the world's wealth. Coach-class passengers say that first-class passengers have created an economic system designed to line their pockets, at the expense of the poor. First-class passengers insist that the accumulation of wealth benefits all passengers, through global aid programs and public charities. Others reject that argument. *To the extent that charity is enabled by the accumulation of surplus wealth [means] it can never be a meaningful solution [to poverty] – for the very processes by which wealth is accumulated are those that produce poverty in the first place.*[201]

Any attempt to determine what God's plan to change the world might look like will require three assumptions in my correspondence. The first assumption is that God will act to protect nature. A corollary of this assumption is that left to our own resources, it's too late to change the direction in which we are traveling. As renowned naturalist David Attenborough points out, the most we can hope for is to slow down the rate at which things get worse. With one or two exceptions, nobody I know seriously believes that global warming can be held at 1.5°C for more than a few years, when bankers have invested nearly $2 trillion to advance coal, oil and gas projects since the Paris Agreement was signed in December 2015.[202] *To stay below 1.5°C we need to keep 93 per cent of known and extractable fossil fuel reserves in the ground. But the Paris Agreement makes no mention of this red line.*[203]

The second assumption in my theory of God's plan to change the world is that the God I am referring to is the God of Abraham and the prophets, because that is the only God I know. Other gods may have a plan to change the world but they are not on my radar, and I doubt they would be so precocious as to invade human history in the way proposed by the Medjugorje apparitions. Each of the Abrahamic beliefs recognize in their own way the unredeemed state of human nature, and in the right circumstances—with the benefit of God's grace—could easily find themselves on the same path to redemption. One scenario I quite like is Jesus coming into land on Jerusalem's Dome of the Rock and being recognized as the promised Messiah by Jews; as Jesus of the Second Coming (the Parousia) by Christians; and by Muslims as Jesus the Prophet who escaped death. That would be a beautiful thing, Holy Father, but not one, I suppose, likely to happen anytime soon.

The third assumption in my theory is that God's plan to change the world—at this moment in history—has nothing to do with the Last Days, the End Times, the Parousia, the Rapture, Armageddon, or the Apocalypse; and everything to do with a new outpouring of the Holy Spirit in a Second Pentecost, leading to a new era of peace. Christians know what a new outpouring of the Holy Spirit will look like from the First Pentecost. *Scripture emphasizes two groups of blessings that the Holy Spirit gives to those who receive him.*[204] The first group of blessings is the seven 'Gifts of the

Holy Spirit' named by the prophet Isaiah: wisdom, under-standing, counsel, fortitude, knowledge, piety, and fear of the Lord (Isa 11:1-3). The second group is the twelve 'Fruits of the Holy Spirit' that the Apostle Paul named in his letter to the Galatians: love, joy, peace, patience, kindness, good-ness, generosity, gentleness, faithfulness, modesty, self-control, and chastity (Gal 5:22-3).

St Louis de Montfort [1673-1716] wrote that the Holy Spirit became fruitful through Mary whom he espoused. *To his faithful spouse, Mary, the Holy Spirit has communicated his ineffable gifts, and he has chosen her to dispense all that he possesses.*[205] While Mary is not the architect of God's plan to change the world, she has a significant role to play as chief engineer, and as the woman clothed with the sun who lives in the blinding light of God through the power of the Holy Spirit.

Early in my pilgrimage, I was astonished to read reports of Mary's message to Marija Pavlovic-Lunetti on June 25, 2019. *I am preparing you for the new times that you may be firm in faith and persevering in prayer, so that the Holy Spir-it may work through you and renew the face of the earth.*[206] Around the same time, I discovered several modern writers, one of whom described *a new presence of the Holy Spirit in the human spirit revealed... at the threshold of the third mil-lennium.*[207]

Italian priest Don Stefano Gobbi [1930-2011] purport-edly received locutions from Mary, and although the locutions never gained official recognition in the Church, they enjoy good standing in religious communities and prayer groups, such as the Mary of the Angelus Community in Australia. These locutions allow an insight into the relationship between Mary and the new outpouring of the Holy Spirit—reminiscent of the work of St Maximilian Kolbe. Fr Gobbi recorded his locutions in a compilation known as the 'Blue Book', where he wrote down what he said were Mary's prophetic words between July 1973 and December 1997. Much of what Fr Gobbi wrote related to the miracle of the Second Pentecost. *It will come with the triumph of my Immaculate Heart in the world. Only then will you see how the tongues of fire of the Spirit of Love will renew the whole world, which will become transformed by the greatest manifestation of Divine Mercy.* [208]

Mary first appeared at Medjugorje on June 24, 1981, the feast day of St John the Baptist, to prepare the way for the Holy Spirit—as the Baptist had done for her son at the river Jordan. Following Jesus' Baptism, he was at prayer when heaven opened and the Holy Spirit descended on him in a physical form, like a dove (Lk 3:21-2). At Medjugorje, Mary encourages us to be open to the Holy Spirit, because God wishes to infuse love in our hearts. Only a heart filled with the Holy Spirit is capable of the kind of love that sees perfection in every person. *'You cannot consider yourself a true believer'*, Our Lady said, *'if you do not see Jesus in every person you meet'.* [209]

On the first day Mary spoke to the children, June 25, 1981, her departing words were *Go in the peace of God.*[210] Six weeks later, she announced herself as the Queen of Peace, and then the word 'Peace' in Croatian began appearing intermittently in the sky over the Medjugorje village. God's plan to change the world is to invade humanity with the Holy Spirit in a Second Pentecost, a package deal comprising the personal and charismatic gifts identified at the First Pentecost as well as the unconditional gifts of love and peace.

A fair question at the end of this letter, Holy Father, is when might we expect to receive the gifts of the Holy Spirit? In one of my earlier letters, I reported on a discussion in Canberra with Fr Emil Milat, a devoted priest whose parents migrated to Australia from Croatia. The priest reminded me that the Judeo-Christian faith is made up of three distinct eras. In the third era, the prophet Mary prepares us for 'God the Holy Spirit' in a Second Pentecost. Our prayers over the centuries in the Lord's Prayer—for God's will to be done and for God's kingdom to come on Earth—will be answered with this new outpouring of the Holy Spirit. The third era was announced just over 100 years ago at Fatima, when Mary promised her heart would triumph. The prophecy will be fulfilled at Medjugorje with Mary's last apparitions. As the secrets are revealed, the Holy Spirit will begin to change the world as we know it.

Three of the visionaries—Mirjana, Ivanka and Jakov—have all ten secrets. The other three—Vicka, Marija and Ivan—have nine of the ten. But nobody knows when the tenth secret will be revealed to the second three. Some commentators have pointed out that the middle of the year 2021 marks the 40th year of the Medjugorje apparitions, recognizing the importance of the number 40 in Judeo-Christian history—so often synonymous with a period of testing and affliction. The Israelites wandered in the desert for 40 years after leaving Egypt before reaching the Promised Land. Moses spent 40 days on Mt Sinai before God gave him the Ten Commandments. In the Book of Judges, the people of Israel were captured by the Philistines for 40 years. Noah's flood ended after 40 days. Jesus' temptation in the desert lasted for 40 days. He ascended to heaven 40 days after the resurrection. Easter begins with Ash Wednesday, followed by 40 days of fasting. And of course, Mary appeared in apparition for the first time in the year 40 CE.

Only the three visionaries—Mirjana, Ivanka and Jakov—can tell us whether anything significant will happen 40 years after the beginning of the Medjugorje apparitions. We will all know soon enough, Holy Father, like it or not. All six visionaries are young enough to live another 40 years, if it pleases God to delay revelation of the secrets—we do not know the timeframe for the secrets to unfold. Wayne Weible said the *hardest unbelievers* will have time to convert during the first three secrets or warnings which *will leave no doubt that God is real and that Mary has come in apparition for the last time.*[211] Wayne understood that revelation of the secrets and their fulfillment would cause a *purification of the world [meaning] more than just the cleansing of the waters and the pollution of the air [but also] a purification of the soul.*[212]

In summary, we know what the gifts of the Holy Spirit will look like from the experience of the First Pentecost, but when we can expect the Second Pentecost is not so certain. Some of us will take comfort from James the Apostle, who said that the wisdom that comes down from above is full of mercy and shows itself by doing good. The peace shown by peacemakers brings a harvest of justice (James 3:17-18). Many of us though are disillusioned—or simply impatient for justice. We can barely conceive of a survival plan let alone a new age of the Holy Spirit and a period of peace that is palpable. Our gloomy expectations are based on the evidence in the natural world—life as we know it is unsustainable and therefore coming to an end. A sense of doom has taken hold because we seem to be incapable of making the changes necessary to survive. And yet our instinct to survive demands that we contemplate the mercy of God delivered sensationally through the intercession of the woman most blessed—and somehow still among us.

Sincerely

Peter Breen

Prodigal Pilgrim Group

Pilgrim Letter 20
World Peace and Mary's Triumph Over Evil

Prodigal Pilgrim Group

Hotel Sulic

Vukovarska 13

Medjugorje

Bosnia & Herzegovina

November 4, 2019

Fr Jorge Mario Bergoglio

Holy Father Pope Francis

Papal Residence

Domus Sanctae Marthae

00120 Citta del Vaticano

Dear Fr Jorge

On this the last day of my pilgrimage, I have a strong sense that Mary is offering humanity a lifeline—an alternative to David Attenborough's observation that things can only get worse. Many people I know believe we are in the process of reaping a whirlwind from the damage done to our civilization because of the injustices we tolerated and the exploitation of limited resources we allowed in the name of economic growth. Mary says we can help reduce the worst of the destructive consequences of this vainglory by changing the way we live and making sacrifices for the benefit of others. How we might do this without God's help was always going to be the sixty-four-dollar question.

Unlike the wedding hosts at Cana in Galilee, I have not kept the good wine till last. On the contrary, I began this pilgrimage fully expecting to discover what Mary's triumph would look like. And now I am ending the journey with the realization that my goal still eludes me. The most I can say is that the triumph of Mary's heart seems likely to manifest as a world without evil.

I asked a fellow pilgrim, a God-fearing conservationist, to consider what the world would look like if Mary were to convince God to flick a switch in every climate contrarian's brain, thereby converting climate science deniers and skeptics to supporters. My fellow pilgrim said that any hypothetical 'flick of a switch' from the other side raised a serious problem, since none of us is obliged to subscribe to climate science; compelling deniers and skeptics to do so could just as easily make them more opposed to the idea— even antipathetic. What we may need is disastrous evidence that cataclysmic climate change is now locked into the natural law (its cause no longer relevant) which does not allow any exceptions for free will other than a miracle.

I asked the conservationist what the absence of evil in the world might look like, and in her opinion, it would mean everyone had an open mind about the possibility that things can only get worse for the Earth. How much worse would not be difficult to imagine—rising sea levels, increasing atmospheric and ocean temperatures, loss of rainforests and loss of biodiversity in the sea and on land. *Up to 140,000 species of plants and animals are disappearing each year due to our over-exploitation of the Earth's ecosystems [which is happening] so fast that scientists have classed this as the sixth mass extinction event in history, with the last one having occurred some 66 million years ago.*[213]

Even if we were ultimately to succeed in eradicating poverty—the hope of every decent person alive—without at the same time drastically reducing consumption in rich countries, then that would be a disaster for the natural environment. A big majority of climate scientists agree that nature has reached a point where it could easily be overwhelmed by human industrial activity. In those circumstances, the precautionary principle should demand that action be taken to protect nature before it's too late. On our present trajectory, the Earth is likely to be 3°C warmer than pre-industrial times by 2100, according to a respected Australian policy paper, causing environmental and social chaos of biblical proportions. More than a billion people would need to be relocated, with a *high likelihood* of civilization as we know it coming to an end.[214]

I spoke again with the conservationist pilgrim and asked what the world would look like if Mary convinced

God to flick a switch in all economists' brains, so they balanced supply and demand of scarce resources. The conservationist said that the primary concern of the economists she knew was the bottom line; and the absence of evil in the world would mean none of us would be trying to profit from scarce resources. *Scientists tell us that even at the existing levels of aggregate global consumption we are already overshooting our planet's ecological capacity by about 60 per cent each year ... To get a sense of how extreme this overconsumption is, if we were all to live like the average citizen of the average high-income country, we would require the ecological capacity equivalent to 3.4 Earths.*[215]

Large corporations (nearly 75 per cent of the world's largest economies) and governments rich and poor, strive for economic growth year after year, irrespective of whether that growth is destructive of the Earth. GDP growth rates of at least 2-3 per cent each year are what we need for a healthy economy, according to the usual industry and government media release. The multiplier effect of compound growth at 4.5 per cent per year—the economist's dream growth figure—means everything doubles every sixteen years with absurd implications. *It doesn't take a scientist to realize that endless exponential growth is absurd, in the true sense of the word. To imagine that we can continue this trajectory indefinitely is to disavow the most obvious truths about our planet's material limits.*[216]

When David Attenborough says things can only get worse, he is talking about potential destruction of the natural world on a scale almost beyond comprehension, while the adjustments we can make to our personal ecological footprints are miniscule by comparison. But we could make some effort to reduce our impact on nature by changing our lifestyles. And apparently most of us pray one way or another, so we could also ask Mary to intercede on our behalf, and remind God in the nicest possible way that we love the natural world, and we do not want the destructive tendencies of human nature and other forces of evil to ruin the Earth. Many of us believe we were supposed to be the Earth's custodians, not its destroyers.

Your predecessor, Pope Benedict XVI, was concerned that reason and religion have parted company in modern times, their differences subsumed by the politics of fake news and misrepresentations of truth and falsity. Benedict said that reason alone has never had the capacity to answer the big questions of human existence. The role of religion is to integrate humanity in its entirety, *to unite feeling, understanding and will and to mediate between them, and to offer some answer to the demand made by everything as a whole ... of society and myself, of present and future.*[217] Benedict concluded: Neither humanity nor the world *can be saved unless God reappears in a convincing fashion.*[218] Joseph Iannuzzi reassures us: Since God sent his only Son to save the world, *it follows that he will indeed save it.*[219]

As the prophet exemplar and spiritual intercessor between God and humanity, Mary allows us to look forward to the transformation of the Earth rather than bear witness to its destruction. No angel or saint is better placed to intercede and mediate with God on our behalf than the woman who has been on the case for humanity since agreeing to carry Jesus in her womb. Her presence in the modern Church, as you know, is recognized in the conciliar documents of the Second Vatican Ecumenical Council. The dogmatic constitution *Lumen Gentium* ('Light of the Nations') says that a new economy was established when the Son of God took a human nature from Mary.[220] What Mary has promised to do—and has demonstrated through 2,000 years of history that she has the capacity to do—is to change the mind of God, so to speak, following her intercession on our behalf.

It seems to me, Holy Father, that Mary is so uniquely placed through her intimacy with the Holy Spirit that God can no more ignore her supplications than ignore what the Apostle Paul described as the groanings of the Spirit. The prayers that the Spirit makes for God's holy people are always in accordance with the mind of God (Rom 8:26). At Medjugorje, Mary foreshadows divine intervention in human affairs through the Holy Spirit, urging her son to work in ways that do not appear to be part of God's plan. The seventh secret comes to mind, the force of which was reduced following her negotiations with God on behalf of

Mirjana, who was suffering over the dire consequences of what was being prophesied. Another example is the large number of Jesus' healing miracles—at Medjugorje and at all the Marian shrines—which were prompted by Mary's intercessions on behalf of sick people. And her last words in Scripture at the wedding feast of Cana may be the best example of the extent of her influence. Ignoring Jesus' objections, Mary asked the wedding servants to do whatever he told them to do (Jn 2:5). It seems that Mary can change God's mind—even down to the catering arrangements—when she is moved to intercede on our behalf.

The expert on the relationship between Mary and the Holy Spirit, St Maximilian Kolbe, said in his notes for a book that 'Spouse of the Holy Spirit' is far from adequate to express the life of the Spirit in and through Mary. *In Jesus there are two natures, divine and human, but one single Person who is God; here on the contrary, we have two natures and two persons, the Holy Spirit and the Immaculata [Mary], but united in a union that defies all human expression.*[221] In spite of the language difficulties, it seems to me that when Mary says her heart will triumph, she speaks with the same Spirit of love and peace that God will disseminate during the Second Pentecost.

Since first visiting Fatima in 1990, I have had a sense that the triumph of Mary's heart will be the triumph of good over evil, although I could never find a satisfactory authority for that idea. Biblical references to the woman and the snake in Genesis (3:15) and the woman and the dragon in Revelation (12:17) were helpful, but they required readers to fill in the allegorical blank spaces. To my knowledge, Mary has never said what the triumph of her heart will look like, although she did seem to be saying that Fatima and Medjugorje were both part of the same plan. *What I started in Fatima I will complete in Medjugorje. My heart will triumph.*[222] In an interview for a book published in 2016, the visionary, Vicka Mijatovic, was asked what it was that Mary needed to finish at Medjugorje? Vicka said, *I believe it's about the hearts of Jesus and Mary winning over evil, but I cannot tell you anything else.*[223]

If Vicka is right, then what we can look forward to is a world with no evil—either defeated or won over to the good—as well as one more answer to our pleading in the Lord's Prayer when we have asked God in every age of Christianity to deliver us from evil. In her messages at Medjugorje, Mary has said that Satan wants to destroy humanity and our natural environment, but God will hear our prayers and give us peace. As descendants of Adam and Eve—fallen humanity—our lot seems to be to share the punishment of our ancestors as well as our living space here on Earth with the forces of evil. I am reminded that Scripture attributes evil in the world to those fallen angels hurled down to the Earth with Satan (Rev 12:1-17). I suspect we have more in common with our fellow exiles than we realize, but we are not really in their league. As you said in a radio broadcast early in your papacy, Holy Father, *only God can look into the face of evil and overcome it.*[224]

At some point, though, we will need God's grace if we are to take a stand against evil and experience real conversion. Spiritual writer and priest, Richard Rohr, talks about personal transformation, reminding us that Jesus said we must die to self if we are to find ourselves (Mt 16:25). *Authentic conversion will always feel like dying, and if you are not trained in dying, it just will not happen—unless and until it's forced on you!*[225] Many of us despair that authentic conversion is beyond our reach as a species, which is the real alarm in David Attenborough's observation that things can only get worse. Mary's triumph over evil may be all that stands between life as we know it and the abyss. Attenborough says that we have a decade from 2020 to 2030 before there is no turning back from the diabolical future we have created.

We have reason to hope that God will not abandon us, and that might be a good place to formally end my pilgrimage. Thank you for any time you have given to considering my mail. It was my privilege to have the opportunity to write to you and to place on record my concerns about the natural environment, as well as my great affection for the Marian apparition sites—especially Medjugorje. Tomorrow, I am heading back to New York for a while, and then home to Australia.

Another anniversary of your encyclical on the natural environment, *Laudato Si: On Care of Our Common Home,* is approaching. If an opportunity happened to arise for the laity to attend celebrations in Rome, do keep in mind your faithful servant from the antipodes.

Sincerely
Peter Breen
Prodigal Pilgrim Group

Concluding Letter

Prodigal Pilgrim Group

Mary of the Angelus Community

2 Burringbar Street

Mullumbimby NSW 2482

Australia

December 10, 2020

Fr Jorge Mario Bergoglio

Holy Father Pope Francis

Papal Residence

Domus Sanctae Marthae

00120 Citta del Vaticano

Dear Fr Jorge

A year has passed since my last correspondence—a year of upheaval if ever there was one—in which the coronavirus pandemic swept the world, wreaking havoc on families and economies and forever changing the way we live. Donald Trump's apparent indifference to the virus seems to have cost him the presidency of the United States of America. Even though Joe Biden has won the race for the White House by about seven million popular votes, the world holds its collective breath for Trump to concede defeat. Secretary of State, Mike Pompeo, has just announced that there will be a smooth transition to a second Trump administration, suggesting that Trump has added election defeat to his list of *truths that must be denied* according to *The Guardian* newspaper.[226] I see you have already called President-elect Biden to congratulate him. You must be pleased that a devout Catholic is now the most powerful leader in the free world.

I read online that you spent some coronavirus lockdown time working on you new book, *Let Us Dream*. A copy of the book turned up today (World Day of Peace) at the Mary of the Angelus Community and I read it in one sitting. I greatly enjoyed what you had to say, especially at the end where you described the importance of pilgrimage. All power to your understanding of the pilgrim who *decenters and transcends as a way of moving forward—she goes out from herself, opens herself to a new horizon, and when she comes home she is no longer the same.*[227] A pilgrim experiences some other dimension of the human journey, *a kind of walking ahead* as you describe it.

Before reading the new book, I had visions of you rattling around in St Peter's Basilica, the Sistine Chapel, and the Vatican Museums during the coronavirus lockdown, looking for all the things you have heard or read about over the years but never had the opportunity to examine in detail, due to the crush of tourists arriving on your doorstep every day. Time alone in the Vatican sounds like heaven on a stick to me, especially if there is no exposure to coronavirus. It may be that you have also found some time during the lockdown to look at my pilgrimage letters, or to further consider the Medjugorje apparitions.

In one of my previous letters, I promised to write to you again, when a decision was made by Australia's High Court in the case of George Cardinal Pell's convictions for child sex abuse offences. Well, as you know, the fateful day arrived earlier this year, and George was acquitted of all convictions—a unanimous decision of the seven High Court judges. I read online that you prayed for innocent convicts wrongly sentenced to prison, which I assume was a thumbs-up for George. None of the lawyers I know were surprised by the decision although some sections of the Australian media still think poor George is Frankenstein with little understanding of the role they played in creating the monster. Nobody in the media has apologized to George.

George seemed to be upbeat when he was ambushed by television journalists at a roadhouse on his way home from his Melbourne prison cell to Sydney. I recognized his characteristic good humor as he apologized to the media for looking like a dag in grandfather cardigan and trouser braces. After a few months in Sydney putting the finishing touches to the first volume of his memoir, *Prison Journal*, George is now back in Rome, as you know, making plans for his book launch in a couple of weeks. Given his wrongful convictions and unjust suffering, it's probably time to forgive His Eminence for his double standards on the existence of hell and the primacy of conscience, although the jury's still out on his antipathy to climate science. Have you ever considered giving George the good oil, Holy Father, by infallibly declaring that climate science is a matter of faith and morals?

By the way, you will be interested in a report just published by Australia's weather and scientific agencies titled *State of the Climate 2020*[228] which confirms that the climate Down Under has warmed by an average of nearly 1.5°C since 1910. The hottest year on record was 2019. Sea levels have risen 25 centimeters since 1880—currently increasing by 3.5 centimeters each decade. Like the rest of the world, Australia is on track to be 3°C hotter than pre-industrial levels by 2100, but unlike the rest of the developed world, Australians remain joined at the hip to the coal and gas industries.

Of great concern is that Greenland, the world's largest island, is melting at the rate of 280 billion tons of ice each year due to global warming, and after the melt, sea levels will be seven meters higher.[229] My first reaction to this statistic was disbelief, until I watched David Attenborough's new film, *Breaking Boundaries: the Science of our Planet*, and learned that Greenland's ice is two miles thick.

I enjoyed the prayers you wrote in April, urging us to seek refuge in the Mother of God during the month of May and in the remaining time of coronavirus, when there is so much anxiety and suffering in the world. You emphasized the need *to alleviate countless situations of poverty* and to invest in medical research instead of *developing and stockpiling arms.* [230] These are my kind of prayers, Holy Father, asking God to confront what seem to me to be the most dangerous forces of evil in the world: poverty, uncontrolled population growth, over-consumption in rich countries and human-induced climate change, all working together to bring down life as we know it.

You may have read the March 25, 2020, message at Medjugorje: *Little children, permit for God to speak to your heart because Satan is reigning and wants to destroy your lives and the earth on which you walk.* Also in March, Mirjana Soldo received the last of her second of the month apparitions from Mary, so things are moving right along at Medjugorje. Little is known about when the apparitions will end.

As much as I would like to continue this correspondence, it feels like I should sign off for the last time. I wish I could say that my faith is stronger at the end of the pilgrimage, but the truth is I remain mystified that God favors some people with strong beliefs—not to mention mutually exclusive strong beliefs—while others believe nothing. My faith remains cautious. The fact is that belief and truth do not always inhabit the same universe, and when they do, why is the truth so hard to come by? I worry that even if the visible and permanent sign at Medjugorje is irrefutable proof that God exists, the Rudy Giuliani principle that truth is not the truth may yet prevail.

If my letters have sparked your interest in Medjugorje, one additional matter comes to mind, and that is the positive implications for the natural environment if you were to lend your personal support to the apparitions—notwithstanding that Vatican bureaucrats are unconvinced about Mary's earthly appearances. You could raise a special prayer intention in the year of the fifth anniversary of *Laudato Si*, and there is no reason to think people of other religions would not accept an invitation to join in prayers directed to protecting our common home.

Just say for a moment that you were to seek guidance from the Holy Spirit about the Medjugorje apparitions and officially announce your intention to do so. Everyone could pray for your enlightenment. A just and merciful God is unlikely to ignore, say, a billion prayers, and may even give you a sign—either direct or through Mary and the Medjugorje visionaries. At least two of your predecessors received signs about Fatima, so are you any less worthy? Of course, it's not for me to tell you how to pray or to organize your life, but if you could somehow get all those people who value your insights to ask God to protect the natural environment when the Medjugorje secrets are finally revealed, then that would be a contribution worthy of the greatest of saints. You are more likely than anyone else I know to find God's favour in your prayers.

May I leave you with the words of brave Mirjana Soldo, the visionary charged with revealing the prophesied events three days before they happen. *Our Lady told me many things that I cannot yet reveal. For now, I can only hint at what our future holds, but I do see indications that the events are already in motion. Things are slowly starting to develop. As Our Lady says, look at the signs of the times, and pray.*[231]

Sincerely
Peter Breen
Prodigal Pilgrim Group

Post Scriptum 1

Family and Other Loved Ones

Prodigal Pilgrim Group

Mary of the Angelus Community

2 Burringbar Street

Mullumbimby NSW 2482

Australia

June 25, 2021

Fr Jorge Mario Bergoglio

Holy Father Pope Francis

Papal Residence

Domus Sanctae Marthae

00120 Citta del Vaticano

Dear Fr Jorge

I received an encouraging letter from Monsignor Roberto Cona at the Vatican Secretary of State office (copy attached for ease of reference). While I was hoping for a letter from you, I remain grateful for small mercies. I am especially grateful to receive your Apostolic Blessing, which you extended to my *family and other loved ones* through the monsignor. Perhaps this was the last of such blessings given the surprise decision of the Congregation for the Doctrine of the Faith just two months ago to exclude same-sex couples from ecclesial blessings.

You may not know that quite a few of my *family and other loved ones* are living in same-sex couple relationships—now judged by the CDF as 'disordered relationships'. *The presence in such relationships of positive elements... cannot justify the relationships and render them legitimate objects of an ecclesial blessing, since the positive elements exist within the context of a union not ordered to the Creator's plan.*[232] Although this statement may be nothing more than one more crisis of faith for the endlessly faithful to deal with, it does feel like an attack on the human dignity of my *family and other loved ones*.

Was it really your intention not to extend your Apostolic Blessing to my brothers and sisters who happen to be gay or lesbian? Of my seven siblings, at least one of them has been in a same-sex couple relationship for nearly 50 years, and their partner is no less a part of the family than the rest of us. Someone else to whom I am related by marriage is intersex—they were born with both male and female genitalia. The CDF assumes, wrongly, that sexuality is simply a matter of choice, and that the creator is always predictable. Are the Vatican bureaucrats able to say whether a relationship with an intersex person is worthy of an ecclesial blessing? Of course, the question is grossly offensive, and yet it appears to be one the Church has overlooked. A more cynical view is that trans issues represent *a new frontier of Catholic bigotry*[233] in which the Church seems to revel in condemnation.

To question a person's sexual identity and their family relationships is to dehumanize them in my opinion, and to align with the forces of evil that seek to do them harm. Suicidal tendencies and the suicide rate are much higher among people suffering from a gender identity crisis than the general population. Nearly half of transgender Australians have attempted suicide.[234] It's a serious problem to be treated sensitively.

According to a recent edition of the Jesuit magazine *America*, it may be that you did not actually approve publication of the CDF ruling, which comes as no surprise to me. The pontiff I know would be unlikely to authorize a document that says gay and lesbian unions are *not ordered to the Creator's plan*. Of course, the Church can bless couples in any relationship it pleases, so why not publish a 'correctione' that says—after consulting the 'sensus fidelium'—you now realize that if a boat or a racehorse can be blessed then there is no reason not to bless same-sex couples. You will recall that the people of Australia in a plebiscite voted 62 per cent in favor of same-sex marriage—the identical result of a national plebiscite in the Republic of Ireland on the same question.

On a related matter (complex questions of human sexuality that the Church oversimplifies), I see that abortion is back in the news for no good reason other than to embarrass the new president. Some members of the US Catholic bishop's conference would deny Joe Biden access to communion because of their perception that he publicly advocates abortion rights. Personally, I was glad to see the back of his predecessor, but some of my Catholic friends lament the 'fact' that Donald Trump was pro-life while Joe Biden, they say, is not—even though Biden is supposed to be a devout Catholic. Like the outspoken members of the bishop's conference, my friends worry about what Biden might do to make the abortion procedure more accessible.

What my friends sometimes forget—or fail to comprehend in the first place—is that the president is personally opposed to abortion. He said so in his excellent 2007 book *Promises to Keep*. He is especially appalled by late term abortion. In 2006, he called himself *the odd man out* in his party, because he did not support federal abortion funding, and voted for bans on the procedure late in pregnancy. As I mentioned in an earlier letter from Lourdes, Trump was pro-life in the run-up to the 2016 election only to the extent that he promised to appoint conservative judges to the Supreme Court in return for financial support from people connected with wealthy political donors. It was a smart political ploy that helped get Trump elected, but weaponizing abortion for political purposes is a sordid business.

Meanwhile, Holy Father, you might want to mention to the faithful that Joe Biden is entitled to live his faith without being harassed by the US bishops—the same men who promote the big lie that the number one social justice issue is the destruction of the unborn in the womb. Other than their credibility, it costs the bishops nothing to keep repeating the lie, while the real number one social justice issue, poverty, costs serious money to alleviate. Too many of us in the Church have a siege mentality about what we believe, refusing to accept the possibility of change even to the point of contemplating schism as a reasonable alternative to tolerating faith practices that offend our opinions and beliefs. In one of her first appearances to the children at Medjugorje in June 1981, Mary wept as she told the children that *Peace must reign between mankind and God and among all people.*[235] But how can we reconcile our differences?

Just two days ago, you gave an excellent homily in the San Damaso Courtyard of the Vatican Apostolic Palace when you introduced a new cycle of catechesis focused on the Apostle Paul's letter to the Galatians. You said that the letter deals with some very important themes for the faith such as freedom, grace and the Christian way of life, and you observed that Paul seemed to be writing for our times.

> *Today too, as then, there is a temptation to close oneself up in some of the certainties acquired in past traditions... Faced with preaching the Gospel that makes us free, that makes us joyful, [some] people are rigid. Always the rigidity: you must do this you must do that...*

Ultimately, faith in the Holy Spirit present in the Church carries us forward and will save us.[236]

You could have been talking about the Church more generally, although I hear on the grapevine that you had the Traditional Latin Mass in your crosshairs. While I understand your reasoning—that Mass in the old form is divisive—for many Catholics it is often their only spiritual refuge from what they see as a secular world gone mad in the absence of God. Tolerance is a two-way street and we all have our beliefs.

Of greater concern in other factions of the Church is discrimination, first perpetrated in the early Church by the Apostle Paul, who failed to recognise the pivotal role women played in the life of Jesus—especially as the first witnesses to the resurrection. Many of us comprising the 'sensus fidelium' feel unrepresented in the Church and struggle with our faith when we view it through the prism of democracy and human rights principles such as justice, equality and freedom from discrimination.

The thing about a democracy is that everyone gets to have their own opinions and beliefs, and there is a sense in which—if you will excuse the vernacular —51 per cent of the people get to screw over the other 49 per cent. Freedom and joyfulness can be vulgar in a democracy, but they also encourage tolerance in that we learn to live with minorities, including minority views about how the world goes around.

More of us than ever need protections afforded to minorities now that politicians—like Church leaders—have become less representative of constituents.

Protecting minorities will become increasingly important for the Christian community over the next few years as the number of Americans who profess to believe in God as described in the Bible slips below 50 per cent. In other countries such as Australia, powerful minority groups with a disproportionate influence on government have perversely decided that self-interest trumps sustainability, threatening the rule of law that underpins every democratic state.

At the end of my letter-writing journey, I find myself looking again at the *USA Today* press clipping advertisement from the Billy Graham Evangelistic Association—only God can fix our problems. And, more relevant than ever, Pope Benedict XVI's insightful observation that neither humanity nor the world can be saved unless God reappears in a convincing fashion. Abraham and the prophets knew what to do because God spoke to them directly, shaping their lives and illuminating the way ahead. Today the world is suffering an existential crisis and many of us believe that the voice of God was never more compelling.

As I said in my previous letters, I could be wrong about my belief. It could be the product of childhood indoctrination, delusional thinking, or some genetic disorder—the religion gene. Meanwhile, I believe in faith (because I can-

not prove it) that Mary is the prophet of our times, and today I looked forward to her monthly message for the world
delivered on the 40th anniversary of the Medjugorje apparitions. Included at the end of the message was the following:
*Therefore, choose God for the good of the land which God
has given you.* An alternative translation of this part of the
message reads: *Therefore, choose God so that it goes well for
you and for the good of the land which God has given you.*

Elsewhere in the message (the full text follows) Mary
urges us to pray for peace and freedom, using language
similar to the words of your homily at the Vatican two days
ago. Whatever the outcome of the extraordinary events at
Medjugorje, the good news, Holy Father, is that you and
Mary seem to be on the case for both the natural environment and humanity. I will be fascinated to see how that potential conflict of interests is resolved. If you have a chance,
you might ask Pope Benedict XVI whether he thinks humanity and the world can both be saved if convincing evidence that God exists turns up at Medjugorje.

In an ominous sign of the times, a heat dome weather
system just settled over the northern hemisphere, causing
temperatures in Canada's British Columbia to rise to 46.6
°C, busting the previous record by a staggering 5 °C. Wild-
fires are burning so intensely in the USA as to create their
own pyro-cumulus storms. In California's Death Valley, the
temperature rose to a deadly 54.5 °C, which may be a modern world record weather event. Pilgrims report today from

Medjugorje that the temperature nudged 40 °C. It was not the number 40 in Judeo-Christian history I had anticipated on the 40th anniversary of the apparitions.

On that note, I really must end this correspondence, unless of course you want additional feedback, which I would be delighted to provide. Do let me know, either directly or through Monsignor Roberto Cona. There is plenty to talk about—especially if you wish to explore further aspects of the Medjugorje phenomenon. The commission of inquiry chaired by Camillo Cardinal Ruini has already recommended in 2017 that the Church approve the first seven days of the apparitions. You could announce that nothing has changed at Medjugorje after 40 years, and now you intend completing the approval process, declaring Mary's appearances 'worthy of belief as private revelation'.

Sincerely

Peter Breen

Prodigal Pilgrim Group

Post Scriptum 2

The Pope's Consecration of Russia

Prodigal Pilgrim Group

Mary of the Angelus Community

2 Burringbar Street

Mullumbimby NSW 2482

Australia

March 25, 2022

Fr Jorge Mario Bergoglio

Holy Father Pope Francis

Papal Residence

Domus Sanctae Marthae

00120 Citta del Vaticano

Dear Fr Jorge

In one of my previous letters, written on the United Nations World Day of Peace in 2020, I suggested you embark upon an ambitious program, asking everyone concerned about the natural environment to accept your invitation to join in prayers seeking God's protection. The letter expressed my concern about collateral damage when the Medjugorje secrets are revealed. I could not have imagined at the time that you would be calling on the world's bishops, the faithful and all people of good will to join you in consecrating Russia and Ukraine to the Immaculate Heart of Mary. And yet today, on the feast of Mary's Annunciation—the same day that Pope John Paul II made the consecration of Russia on March 25, 1984—prayer is again the Pope's response to the world facing the prospect of another all-consuming war in Europe. *Acting as the Universal Pastor of the Church, Pope Francis will renew the consecration urged at Fatima more than 100 years ago...We raise our hearts, our minds and our voices to God for an end to this horrific violence and destruction [in Ukraine].* [237]

Like his hero Josef Stalin, who ordered the execution of a million of his own citizens, Vladimir Putin seeks to divide his nation, drawing a distinction between those citizens who are *true patriots* and those who are fifth columnists and traitors—to be *spat out like midges* that fly into the mouths of the Russian people. *I am convinced that such a natural and necessary self-purification of society will strengthen our country, our solidarity, cohesion and readiness to respond to any challenges.* [238]

The Economist magazine rightly calls this language *disconcertingly familiar fascist rhetoric.* [239] You must be concerned, Holy Father, that the Medjugorje prophecies are linked to the Fatima secrets according to Mirjana Soldo, [240] and the conversion of Russia (as in pursuing peace and freedom) is as problematic today as it was in 1917.

If the opportunity arises, you might direct President Putin's attention to Stalin's question: How many divisions does the Pope have? The Pope has a billion strong prayer army with as much firepower as any number of guns and rockets that may exist in the Russian war chest. And today, the Pope is supported by countless millions of internet users fighting a war of words with the people of Russia, informing them that Putin is the enemy—not their fellow citizens or the amorphous West. Here is one exchange I had just last week on social media:

Svetlana Khatueva: *Russia is Orthodox. Churches are full. We're all praying for peace and we're in pain. It's not a war between Russia and Ukraine. It's the operation aimed against NATO's military bases on the Ukrainian territory that got too close to Russia's borders. Putin asked for negotiations in 2021 time and again but western politicians laughed him off. Ukraine's only problem is that NATO chose its territory as the closest to Russia. And now the war is on its territory. In 2014 the west started supporting and funding Ukraine's neo-nationalist forces who have been bombing Donbass since then because Donbass is historically loyal to Russia—people there speak Russian. The world didn't care. People in Donbass have been dying for eight years. Russia's plan is to demilitarize Ukraine and destroy NATO's objects imposing a nuclear threat to Russia. And save people of Donbass.*

Prodigal Pilgrim Group: *You are seriously in error Sveta. There are no NATO military bases, in Donbass or any other part of Ukraine. Ukraine does not qualify for NATO membership. You are propagating the Putin lie that he's waging a military operation when in fact he's invading a sovereign state and starting a war in breach of international law. If you call the so-called military operation a war or invasion in Russia you go to jail for up to 15 years according to a law passed in the Russian Duma last Friday. Writers and journalists are leaving Russia in droves to avoid the wrath of the Putin iron fist. No surprise to me to hear that churches are full. Where else can you go to seek refuge from a war criminal who appears to be to be either bad or mad—and possibly both? It's hard to believe in a civilized world that once again we're looking down the barrel of war in Europe. God help all of us Sveta.*

Svetlana Khatueva: *Churches in Russia have been full for years. This is not my first day in church! And how do you know that what you are saying is true and I'm wrong? It's just something you chose to believe. Well, I have sources from within Ukraine to believe differently. The 'sovereign state' has been an American colony since 2014. New nazis are there. I'm not going to argue with you. Let's not. Clearly we're reading different propaganda stories. Your reading yours and choose to believe it. Instead of taking sides I'd rather we stand and look from above. May God's will be done.*

Prodigal Pilgrim Group: *I know that what I'm saying is true, Sveta, because I live in a free and democratic country where information is not suppressed by the state, and we are not jailed for saying what we think, and we get to vote in free and fair elections for leaders who work for the good of the people, not to enrich themselves and treat their fellow citizens as unwanted dogs. Putin has been in power since Boris Yeltsin tapped him on the shoulder 22 years ago. He has made himself and his oligarchs some of the richest people in the world at the expense of the Russian people. Power corrupts and absolute power corrupts absolutely (with apologies to Lord Acton). The idea that Ukraine is an American colony inhabited by new nazis is simply laughable. Look from above and choose to believe that we're reading different propaganda stories if you must, but history will record Putin as Vlad the Bad (or Mad), as evil and deluded as every other dictator that preceded him.*

It's true that churches are full in Russia—70 per cent of Russians claim allegiance to the Orthodox faith. On one view, that may simply make the dictator Putin's attempt to suborn Christianity to his obscene cause that much more disgusting. Another view is that the European Union and Russia have common roots in Christianity. According to tradition, the Apostle Andrew founded Christianity in Russia, and the Russian Orthodox Church thrived until the Bolshevik revolution of 1917 and the Russian Civil War. Church property was confiscated and believers purged as atheistic communism set about separating church and state. Stalin rehabilitated the church in 1941 for his own purposes—to encourage Russian patriotism through popular Christian belief and to appease the World War II allies who shared Russia's Christian heritage.

Unlike Stalin, Putin is apparently a believer, overtly pious, and perhaps even guided by his spiritual life. He wears his religion around his neck in the form of a baptismal cross on a silver chain that was given to him by his Christian mother and blessed at Jesus' tomb in Jerusalem. Putin also has a staunch ally in Patriarch Kirill of the Russian Orthodox Church, who surprised nobody when he endorsed the attack on Ukraine, blaming the West for undermining the family and promoting gay-pride parades.[241] Putin's war, Kirill said, is a struggle having a metaphysical significance. Nobody knows what happened to 'love thy neighbour' in Russian Christianity, Holy Father. How Christians of any denomination can justify the indiscriminate bombing of women and children is the metaphysical struggle for most of us.

Even if Patriarch Kirill and President Putin do believe they have a brief from God to save the world from decadence and decay, and they share a genuine fear of annihilation at the hands of NATO, Russia's church and state alliance is on the wrong side of human history. Most of us today believe in peace, freedom and fundamental human rights. We have popular support for our belief—whether we arrived at this belief through religion or the secular world, or both. And we are willing to fight to the death for our belief, shoulder to shoulder with the people of Ukraine. *And while we may not be used to questions of what it means to 'believe' ceasing to be academic and becoming matters of life and death, those days may be upon us.* [242]

Finally, I wholeheartedly support your consecration of Russia and Ukraine to the Immaculate Heart of Mary, whether you're personally motivated by the consecration urged at Fatima in 1917, or you simply want to ask God— through Mary—to save us from President Putin. Perhaps you will also have a quiet word seeking God's protection for life on Earth—for the benefit of our children and grandchildren. Long after Putin has met his predictable end, we will still have the existential problem of man-made global warming to deal with, a problem that would benefit greatly from God's intervention in our affairs in the way suggested by your predecessor Pope Benedict XVI—divine reappearance in a convincing fashion. Otherwise, let's hope and pray that God's mercy extends to saving us from ourselves.

Sincerely

Peter Breen

Prodigal Pilgrim Group

Dear children! My heart is joyful because over the years I have seen your love and openness to my call. Today I call on you to pray with me for peace and freedom, because Satan is strong, and with his deceptions, wants to lead as many hearts as possible away from my Motherly Heart. Therefore, choose God so that it goes well for you and for the good of the land which God has given you. Thank you for having responded to my call.

Mary's Message at Medjugorje on June 25, 2021,
the 40th Anniversary of the Apparitions

Dear children! I am with you and we pray together. Help me with prayer, little children, that Satan may not prevail. His power of death, hatred and fear has visited the earth. Therefore, little children, return to God and to prayer, to fasting and to renunciation, for all those who are downtrodden, poor and have no voice in this world without God. Little children, if you do not return to God and His Commandments, you do not have a future. That is why He sent me to you to guide you. Thank you for having responded to my call.

Mary's Message at Medjugorje on February 25, 2022,
the day after Russia began war in Ukraine

I am listening to your cry and prayers for peace. For years, Satan has been fighting for war. That is why God sent me among you to guide you on the way of holiness because humanity is at a crossroads. I am calling you to return to God and to God's Commandments that it may be good for you on earth, and that you may come out of this crisis into which you have entered because you are not listening to God who loves you and desires to save you and lead you to a new life. Thank you for having responded to my call.

Mary's Message at Medjugorje on March 25, 2022,
the feast of the Annunciation, and the day
Pope Francis consecrated Russia and Ukraine

Pope Francis' Consecration of Russia and Ukraine to the Immaculate Heart of Mary on the feast of the Annunciation at St Peter's Basilica, Vatican City March 25, 2022

At this hour, a weary and distraught humanity stands with you beneath the cross, needing to entrust ourselves to you, and through you, to be consecrated to Christ. The people of Ukraine and Russia, who venerate you with great love, now turn to you, even as your heart beats with compassion for them and for all those peoples decimated by war, hunger, injustice and poverty.

Therefore, Mother of God and our Mother, to your Immaculate Heart we solemnly entrust and consecrate ourselves, the Church and all humanity, especially Russia and Ukraine. Accept this act that we carry out with confidence and love. Grant that war may end and peace spread throughout the world...We trust that through your heart, peace will dawn once more. To you we consecrate the future of the whole human family, the needs and expectations of every people, the anxieties and hopes of the world.

Through your intercession, may God's mercy be poured out on the earth and the gentle rhythm of peace return to mark our days. Our Lady of the Annunciation, on whom the Holy Spirit descended, restore among us the harmony that comes from God. May you, our living fountain of hope, water the dryness of our hearts...You once trod the streets of our world; lead us now on the paths of peace. Amen.

Acknowledgements

I wish to thank Milanka Lachman in the USA and Slavenka Jelavic in Medjugorje, tireless pilgrim advisers, translators, and direction finders in the time of coronavirus. Valerie Murphy and Katherine Whitehouse of the Mary of the Angelus Community encouraged me to write the book. Emil Milat and Anselm Okeke both helped me over significant hurdles, enabling me to stay on message. A big thank you to all the Angelus mob, especially Paul Murphy, who found me a quiet place to write, and Anthony Whitten who guided me in cyberspace.

I am exceedingly grateful to my editors, Margie Tubbs and Diane Thomas, as well as the writer Stephanie Dowrick who first looked at this story in another form some 30 years ago. *Prodigal Pilgrim* might not have seen the light of day were it not for the Australian Society of Authors kindly publishing a blurb about it in the *International Marketplace Catalogue*, an unexpected promotion that required me to put an end to my missives and stop harassing the papal secretariat.

A big thank you to my Australian publishers David Hughan and Karen Tayleur at Garratt Publishing in Melbourne, and to Sebastian Mahfood at En Route Books and Media in St Louis, Missouri, USA. *Prodigal Pilgrim* is now published in six countries. A Spanish edition is underway, and Dr Mahfood is determined to place a copy in the hands of Pope Francis. Now that would be some sort of miracle.

My thanks to George Cardinal Pell, who read what I had to say about him, and responded generously. The cardinal sent me a note that he had no problem with what was written, although he was not sure his *view on no-one in hell (as a possibility) is heretical; and the idea that truth rules conscience is as old as Jesus—and older.*[243] The convincing but ultimately unreliable evidence that convicted George Pell is a salutary reminder that subjective belief in an allegation or assertion—regardless of the honesty of the person making it—is not a good basis for deciding that what is being alleged or asserted is true.

I would like to thank my classmates from St Columba's College Seminary at Springwood in the Blue Mountains west of Sydney where I was a student priest in the 1960s. Most of us kept in touch over the years thanks to Zvonimir Gavranovic who maintained a mailing list of the 'blokes' and organized irregular reunions. Peter Marr and Dennis Carroll from the seminary days read early drafts of *Prodigal Pilgrim* and helped me find a narrative voice for the story. My grateful thanks also to Greg and Ann Coonan and Hugh and Mary Thompson for their support and encouragement in the face of endless second thoughts.

One of our favorite teachers at the seminary, Bishop Bede Heather, died earlier this year. He was an enlightened man, honored in a eulogy by Anglican priest, Rod Bower, who said of his friend: *There was something about Bede's presence that somehow raised the bar on our own way of being. When I was with him I wanted to be just a little less judgmental, and just a little more forgiving and understanding.*[244] Bede Heather kept the faith. Could any of us ask for more?

Endnotes

1. Joseph Cardinal Ratzinger, *Truth and Tolerance: Christian Belief and World Religions*, Ignatius Press, San Francisco, CA, USA, 2003, p144.

2. Bertoncello Artigrafiche, *Medjugorje: A Portfolio of Images*, Alba House Press, New York, NY, USA, 1987, p12.

3. Manning Clark, *Selected Documents in Australian History*, vol 2, Angus & Robertson, Sydney NSW, Australia, 1955, p109 cited in Frank Brennan, *Acting on Conscience*, University of Queensland Press, St Lucia Qld, Australia, 2007, p230.

4. Advertisement, 'Special Day of Prayer for the President', Billy Graham Evangelistic Association, *USA Today*, May 2019.

5. Francis Trochu, *Saint Bernadette Soubirous 1844-1879*, Tan Books and Publishers, Rockford, IL, USA, 1985, p42.

6. Ibid. p59.

7. Ibid. p65.

8. Ibid. p105.

9. Ibid.

10. Ibid. p63.

11. Ibid. p157.

12. Ibid. p356.

13. Ibid. p361.

14. Ibid. p384.

15. https://www.pewresearch.org/politics/2019/08/29/u-s-public-continues-to-favor-legal-abortion-oppose-overturning-roe-v-wade/

16. Pope Francis, *Apostolic Exhortation Gaudete et Exsultate*, Holy See, Vatican City State, March 19, 2018, par 101.

17. Alan Schreck, *Your Life in the Holy Spirit*, The Word Among Us Press, Ijamsville, MD, USA, 1995, p159.

18. https://www.pewforum.org/2011/12/19/global-christianity-movements-and-denominations/

19. Pope Francis, 'Address to Catholic Charismatic Renewal Members', Paul VI Audience Hall, Vatican City State, June 8, 2019.

20. Austen Ivereigh, 'Is Francis our first charismatic pope?' *America: the Jesuit Review*, New York, NY, USA, June 2019.

21. Marianne Trouve (ed), *The Sixteen Documents of Vatican II*, Pauline Books, Boston MA, USA, 1999, p239.

22. Catechism of the Catholic Church, Holy See, US Catholic Conference, Washington, DC, 2019, par 1782.

23. Thomas Aquinas, *Summa Theologiae*, Cambridge University Press, New York, NY, USA, 2006, cited in Todd Salzman and Michael Lawler, 'Amoris Laetitia and Catholic Morals', *The Furrow*, Vol 67 No 12, Maynooth, Ireland, December 2016.

24. Catechism of the Catholic Church, Holy See, US Catholic Conference, Washington, DC, 2019, par 1785.

25. Marianne Trouve (ed), *The Sixteen Documents of Vatican II*, Pauline Books, Boston MA, USA, 1999, p493.

26. Catechism of the Catholic Church, Holy See, US Catholic Conference, Washington, DC, 2019, par 389.

27. Frank Brennan, *Acting on Conscience*, University of Queensland Press, St Lucia, Qld, Australia, 2007, p73.

28. Ibid. p236.

29. Ibid. p43.

30. Ibid. p29.

31. Ibid. p228.

32. Catechism of the Catholic Church, Holy See, US Catholic Conference, Washington, DC, 2019, par 971.

33. Ibid. par 717.

34. HM Manteau-Bonamy, *Immaculate Conception and the Holy Spirit*, Franciscan Marytown Press, Libertyville, IL, USA, 2017, p112.

35. Thomas W Petrisko, *The Fatima Prophecies*, St Andrews Productions, McKees Rocks, PA, USA, 1998, p17.

36. John Haffert, 'The Prophecy of Saint Catherine Laboure', *Soul Magazine*, Drums, PA, USA, March-April 1983.

37. Rene Laurentin & Michael Corteville, *Discovery of the Secret of La Salette*, Fayard Publications, Paris, France, 2002, p27.

38. Philip Ziegler, *Militant Grace*, Baker Publishing Group, Grand Rapids, MI, USA, 2018, p107.

39. Emil Milat, Conversations with the author at St Patrick's Church, Canberra, ACT, Australia, 2019.

40. Ibid.

41. Reginald Fuller, *Interpreting the Miracles*, SCM Press, London, England UK, 1976, p8.

42. CS Lewis, *Miracles*, Harper Collins Publishers, London, England UK, 2012, p222-4.

43. Ibid.

44. Brian Catling, *The Erstwhile*, Hodder & Stoughton, London, England, UK, 2018, p66.

45. June Klins, *Medjugorje Newsletter*, Weible Columns Publishing, Hiawassee, GA, USA, Dec 2018, p4-5.

46. www.cradio.org.au/assets/minute-with-mary/MWM-22.2-MaxKolbe-Mary-HolySpirit.mp3

47. HM Manteau-Bonamy, *Immaculate Conception and the Holy Spirit*, Franciscan Marytown Press, Libertyville, IL, USA, 2017, p101.

48. Marianne Trouve (ed), *The Sixteen Documents of Vatican II: Lumen Gentium,* ed Pauline Books & Media, Boston, MA, USA, 1999, p186.

49. HM Manteau-Bonamy, *Immaculate Conception and the Holy Spirit*, Franciscan Marytown Press, Libertyville, IL, USA, 2017, p35.

50. Ibid. p39.

51. Ibid.

52. Ibid. p41.

53. Francis Johnston, *Fatima: The Great Sign*, Augustine Publishing Co, Chulmleigh, Devon, UK, 1980, p29.

54. Antonio Borelli Machado, *Fatima: The Unheeded Message*, TFP Bureau, Sydney NSW, Australia, 2005, p42.

55. Lucia dos Santos, *Fatima in Lucia's Own Words*, Pastoral Secretariat, Fatima, Portugal, 2000, p85.

56. Ibid. p123.

57. Ibid. p124.

58. Ibid. p215.

59. Andrew Apostoli, *Fatima for Today*, Ignatius Press, San Francisco, CA, USA, 2010, p86.

60. Joseph Cardinal Ratzinger, 'The Message of Fatima', *L'Osservatore Romano: Weekly Edition in English*, Special Insert N26, Holy See, Vatican City State, June 28, 2000, p8.

61. Antonio Borelli Machado, *Fatima: The Unheeded Message*, TFP Bureau, Sydney NSW, Australia, 2005, p56.

62. Andrew Apostoli, *Fatima for Today*, Ignatius Press, San Francisco, CA, USA, 2010, p264.

63. Tarcisio Cardinal Bertone, *The Last Secret of Fatima*, Random House Inc, New York, NY, USA, 2008, p64.

64. Foreign Service Institute, 'Milestones', US Department of State, Washington, DC, USA, May 2017, p2.

65. Lenin's Collected Works Vol 26, 'The Russian Revolution', Progress Publishers, Moscow, Russia, 1972, p40.

66. Lucia dos Santos, *Fatima in Lucia's Own Words*, Pastoral Secretariat, Fatima, Portugal, 2000, p124.

67. William Taubman, *Gorbachev: His Life and Times*, Simon & Schuster, London, England, UK, 2017, p685.

68. George Weigel, *Witness to Hope: The Biography of Pope John Paul II*, Harper Collins Publishers, New York, NY, USA, 1999, p834.

69. Andrew Apostoli, *Fatima for Today*, Ignatius Press, San Francisco, CA, USA, 2010, p93.

70. Antonio Borelli Machado, *Fatima: The Unheeded Message*, TFP Bureau, Sydney, NSW, Australia, 2005, p39.

71. Francis Johnston, *Fatima: The Great Sign*, Augustine Publishing Co, Chulmleigh, Devon, UK, 1980, p19.

72. Ibid. p12.

73. Pope Francis, 'Greeting to Pilgrims at the Chapel of Apparitions in the Shrine of Our Lady of Fatima', Holy See Press Office, Vatican City State, May 12, 2017.

74. Francis Johnston, *Fatima: The Great Sign*, Augustine Publishing Co, Chulmleigh, Devon, UK, 1980, p43.

75. Ibid. p44.

76. Lucia dos Santos, *Fatima in Lucia's Own Words*, Pastoral Secretariat, Fatima, Portugal, 2000, p92.

77. Andrew Apostoli, *Fatima for Today*, Ignatius Press, San Francisco, CA, USA, 2010, p104.

78. Lucia dos Santos, *Fatima in Lucia's Own Words*, Pastoral Secretariat, Fatima, Portugal, 2000, p180.

79. Mirjana Soldo, *My Heart Will Triumph*, CatholicShop Publishing, Cocoa FL, USA, 2016, p150.

80. Francis Johnston, *Fatima: The Great Sign*, Augustine Publishing Co, Chulmleigh, Devon, UK, 1980, p46.

81. John de Marchi, *The True Story of Fatima*, The Fatima Center, Buffalo, NY, USA, 2009, p49.

82. Lucia dos Santos, *Fatima in Lucia's Own Words*, Pastoral Secretariat, Fatima, Portugal, 2000, pp180-182.

83. John de Marchi, *The True Story of Fatima*, The Fatima Center, Buffalo, NY, USA, 2009, p49.

84. Ibid.

85. CS Lewis, *The Problem of Pain*, Harper Collins Publishers, London, England, UK, 2002, pp91-4.

86. Ibid. p105.

87. Emil Milat, Conversations with the Author, St Patrick's Church, Canberra, ACT, Australia, 2019.

88. Ibid.

89. Andrew Apostoli, *Fatima for Today*, Ignatius Press, San Francisco, CA, USA, 2010, p120.

90. John de Marchi, *The True Story of Fatima*, The Fatima Center, Buffalo, NY, USA, 2009, p53.

91. Lucia dos Santos, *Fatima in Lucia's Own Words*, Pastoral Secretariat, Fatima, Portugal, 2000, p182.

92. Francis Johnston, *Fatima: The Great Sign*, Augustine Publishing Co, Chulmleigh, Devon, UK, 1980, p51.

93. Ibid. p52.

94. Ibid. p58.

95. John Haffert, *Meet the Witnesses*, AMI Press, Washington, NJ, USA, 1961, p86.

96. Francis Johnston, *Fatima: The Great Sign*, Augustine Publishing Co, Chulmleigh, Devon, UK, 1980, p53.

97. Joseph Pronechen, 'Fatima's little-known miracles with earth and water', *National Catholic Register*, Kettering, OH, USA, Sep 2017, p2.

98. Ibid.

99. John Cornwell, *Powers of Darkness Powers of Light*, Penguin Books, New York, NY, USA, p388.

100. Mirjana Soldo, *My Heart Will Triumph*, CatholicShop Publishing, Cocoa, FL, USA, 2016, p155.

101. Mike Willesee, *A Sceptic's Search for Meaning*, Pan Macmillan, Sydney, NSW, Australia, 2019, pp234-5.

102. Ibid. p249.

103. Ron Tesoriero and Lee Han, *Unseen: The Origin of Life Under the Microscope*, Published by Ron Tesoriero, Kincumber, NSW, Australia, 2013, p240.

104. Joseph A Pelletier, *Our Lady Comes to Garabandal: Including Conchita's Diary*, Workers of Our Lady of Mount Carmel, Lindenhurst, NY, USA, 1971, p38.

105. Ibid. p39.

106. Ibid. p50.

107. Ibid. p176.

108. www.garabandal.us/wp-content/uploads/2013/01/bo_interview_bishop.pdf

109. See also Christopher Ferrara, *Secret Still Hidden*, Good Counsel Publications, Pound Ridge, NY, USA, 2008.

110. Joseph A Pelletier, *Our Lady Comes to Garabandal: Including Conchita's Diary*, Workers of Our Lady of Mount Carmel, Lindenhurst, NY, USA, 1971, p147.

111. Eusebio Garcia de Pesquera, *She Went in Haste to the Mountain*, The Workers of Our Lady of Mount Carmel, Lindenhurst, NY, USA, 2003, p650.

112. Ibid. p649.

113. Pope Francis, *Laudato Si: On Care of Our Common Home*, Holy See, Vatican City State, 2015.

114. Private email to the author from a prayer group claiming to represent 'fervent Catholics and others'

115. Catechism of the Catholic Church, Holy See, US Catholic Conference, Washington, DC, 2019, par 67.

116. Eusebio Garcia de Pesquera, *She Went in Haste to the Mountain*, The Workers of Our Lady of Mount Carmel, Lindenhurst, NY, USA, 2003 p311.

117. Christine Watkins, *The Warning*, Queen of Peace Media, Sacramento CA, USA, 2019 p(i).

118. Ibid. pp243-6.

119. Thomas W Petrisko, *The Miracle of the Illumination of All Consciences*, St Andrew's Productions, McKees Rocks PA, USA, 2000, pp35-6.

120. Christine Watkins, *The Warning*, Queen of Peace Media, Sacramento CA, USA, 2019 p227.

121. Ibid.

122. Ibid. p273.

123. Joey Lomangino, 'The Warning and the Miracle', *Garabandal International Magazine*, The Workers of Our Lady of Mount Carmel, Lindenhurst NY, USA, Oct-Dec 2004, p8.

124. Ibid. p10.

125. Eusebio Garcia de Pesquera, *She Went in Haste to the Mountain*, The Workers of Our Lady of Mount Carmel, Lindenhurst, NY, USA, 2003, p151.

126. CS Lewis, *Miracles*, Harper Collins Publishers, London, England, UK, 2012, p5.

127. Ibid. p94.

128. Ibid. p213.

129. Joseph A Pelletier, *Our Lady Comes to Garabandal: Including Conchita's Diary*, Workers of Our Lady of Mount Carmel, Lindenhurst, NY, USA, 1971 p153.

130. Joey Lomangino, 'The Warning and the Miracle', *Garabandal International Magazine*, The Workers of Our Lady of Mount Carmel, Lindenhurst NY, USA, Oct-Dec 2004, pp10-11.

131. Eusebio Garcia de Pesquera, *She Went in Haste to the Mountain*, The Workers of Our Lady of Mount Carmel, Lindenhurst NY, USA, 2003, p174.

132. Joseph A Pelletier, *Our Lady Comes to Garabandal: Including Conchita's Diary*, Workers of Our Lady of Mount Carmel, Lindenhurst, NY, USA, 1971, p70.

133. Ibid. p156

134. www.mysticsofthechurch.com/2014/06/the-death-of-joey-lomangino-blow-to.html p4.

135. Wayne Weible, *Medjugorje: The Last Apparition – How It Will Change the World*, New Hope Press, Hiawassee GA, USA, 2013, p205.

136. Mirjana Soldo, *My Heart Will Triumph*, CatholicShop Publishing, Cocoa, FL, USA, 2016, p120.

137. Joseph A Pelletier, *Our Lady Comes to Garabandal: Including Conchita's Diary*, Workers of Our Lady of Mount Carmel, Lindenhurst, NY, USA, 1971, p163.

138. Ibid.

139. Eusebio Garcia de Pesquera, *She Went in Haste to the Mountain*, The Workers of Our Lady of Mount Carmel, Lindenhurst NY, USA, 2003, p413.

140. Ibid.

141. Joseph A Pelletier, *Our Lady Comes to Garabandal: Including Conchita's Diary*, Workers of Our Lady of Mount Carmel, Lindenhurst, NY, USA, 1971 p163.

142. Ibid. p165.

143. John Cornwell, *Powers of Darkness Powers of Light*, Penguin Books, New York, NY, USA, 1991, pp171-5.

144. Ibid. pp171-3.

145. Ibid.

146. Ibid. p175.

147. Barry Hanratty, *Garabandal*, Garabandal Journal Publishing, St Cloud, MN, USA, 2018, pp11-12.

148. Ibid. p12.

149. Eusebio Garcia de Pesquera, *She Went in Haste to the Mountain*, The Workers of Our Lady of Mount Carmel, Lindenhurst NY, USA, 2003, p91.

150. Joseph A Pelletier, *Our Lady Comes to Garabandal: Including Conchita's Diary*, Workers of Our Lady of Mount Carmel, Lindenhurst, NY, USA, 1971, p98.

151. John Cornwell, *Powers of Darkness Powers of Light*, Penguin Books, New York, NY, USA, 1991, p389.

152. Nick Donnelly, *Who is the Devil: What Pope Francis Says*, CTC Publications, London UK, 2014, p14.

153. www.theguardian.com/world/2019/mar/01/canada-boreal-forest-toilet-paper-us-climate-change-impact-report.

154. www.smh.com.au/environment/conservation/politicians-have-no-clue-what-effect-adani-will-have-on-water-expert.

155. Pope Francis, *Laudato Si: On Care of Our Common Home*, Holy See, Vatican City State, 2015, p92

156. Nick Donnelly, *Who is the Devil: What Pope Francis Says*, CTC Publications, London UK, 2014, p29.

157. Ibid. p30.

158. Catechism of the Catholic Church, Holy See, US Catholic Conference, Washington, DC, 2019, par 394-5.

159. Ibid. par 404.

160. CS Lewis, *The Screwtape Letters*, Time-Life Books Incorporated, Chicago, Il, USA, 1963, pp xxii-xxiii.

161. The Victorian Court of Appeal dismissed Pell's appeal against his convictions by a 2-1 majority decision on August 21, 2019. An application for leave to appeal the Court of Appeal decision to Australia's High Court was decided on April 7, 2020. All seven judges of the High Court found Cardinal Pell was wrongly convicted, releasing him from prison.

162. George Cardinal Pell, Correspondence to the author from the Polding Centre, Sydney, NSW, Australia, 2012.

163. Ibid.

164. Ibid.

165. Cardinal Pell stands by his views on hell and conscience and denies those views contradict Church teaching. See the acknowledgements p203 at the end of *Prodigal Pilgrim*.

166. Joan Ashton, *The People's Madonna*, Harper Collins Publishers, London, UK, 1991, p101.

167. Mark Miravalle and Wayne Weible, *Are the Medjugorje Apparitions Authentic?* New Hope Press, Hiawassee GA, USA, 2008, p27.

168. Joan Ashton, *The People's Madonna*, Harper Collins Publishers, London, UK, 1991, p100.

169. Janice T Connell, *The Visions of the Children*, St Martin's Press, New York, NY, USA, 1992, p14.

170. Joan Ashton, *The People's Madonna*, Harper Collins Publishers, London, UK, 1991, p45.

171. Ibid. p47.

172. Wayne Weible, *Medjugorje: The Last Apparition - How it Will Change the World*, New Hope Press, Hiawassee, GA, USA, 2013, p208.

173. Mirjana Soldo, *My Heart Will Triumph*, CatholicShop Publishing, Cocoa, FL, USA, 2016, p316.

174. Wayne Weible, *Medjugorje: The Last Apparition - How it Will Change the World*, New Hope Press, Hiawassee, GA, USA, 2013, p208.

175. Ibid. p213.

176. Mario Vasilj, *Medjugorje: Our Lady's Apostles - Mirjana's Testimony*, Ogranak Matice Hrvatske, Citluk Medjugorje, Bosnia & Herzegovina, 2015, p48.

177. Mirjana Soldo, *My Heart Will Triumph*, CatholicShop Publishing, Cocoa FL, USA, 2016, pp367.

178. Mario Vasilj, *Medjugorje: Our Lady's Apostles - Mirjana's Testimony*, Ogranak Matice Hrvatske, Citluk Medjugorje, Bosnia & Herzegovina, 2015, p48.

179. Wayne Weible, *Medjugorje: The Last Apparition - How it Will Change the World*, New Hope Press, Hiawassee GA, USA, 2013, p214.

180. Barry Hanratty, *Garabandal*, Garabandal Journal Publishing, St Cloud MN, USA, 2018, p49.

181. Wayne Weible, *Medjugorje: The Last Apparition*, New Hope Press, Hiawassee, GA, USA, 2013, p215.

182. Ibid. p227.

183. Steve Shawl, *The Medjugorje Messages*, Medjugorje Web, DeKalb IL, USA, 2019, p219.

184. Mirjana Soldo, *My Heart Will Triumph*, CatholicShop Publishing, Cocoa, FL, USA, 2016, p367.

185. Pope Francis with Dominique Wolton, *The Path to Change*, Bluebird Books, London, UK, 2018, p177.

186. Mirjana Soldo, *My Heart Will Triumph*, CatholicShop Publishing, Cocoa, FL, USA, 2016, p317.

187. Catechism of the Catholic Church, Holy See, US Catholic Conference, Washington, DC, 2019, par 1449.

188. It took some time for the author to arrive at this understanding. See Mary's message to Marija Pavlovic-Lunetti at Medjugorje on Apr 25, 2020.

189. Mirjana Soldo, *My Heart Will Triumph*, CatholicShop Publishing, Cocoa, FL, USA, 2016, p137.

190. Ibid. p138.

191. Mario Vasilj, *Medjugorje: Our Lady's Apostles – Mirjana's Testimony*, Ogranak Matice Hrvatske, Citluk Medjugorje, Bosnia & Herzegovina, 2015, p78.

192. Ibid. pp80-1.

193. Mirjana Soldo, *My Heart Will Triumph*, CatholicShop Publishing, Cocoa, FL, USA, 2016, p327.

194. Ibid. p325.

195. Ibid. p191.

196. Ibid. p196.

197. Pope Francis, *The Church of Mercy: A Vision for the Church*, Loyola Press, Chicago, IL, USA, 2014, p76.

198. Mirjana Soldo, *My Heart Will Triumph*, CatholicShop Publishing, Cocoa, FL, USA, 2016, p28.

199. Ibid. p231.

200. Ibid. p279.

201. Jason Hickel, *The Divide: A Brief Guide to Global Inequality and its Solutions*, William Heinemann Publishers, London, England, UK, 2017, p256.

202. Patrick Greenfield, 'Top investment banks provide billions to expand fossil fuel industry', *The Guardian*, London, England, UK, October 13, 2019.

203. Jason Hickel, *The Divide: A Brief Guide to Global Inequality and its Solutions*, William Heinemann Publishers, London, England, UK, 2017, p247.

204. Peter Cameron, *The Gifts of the Holy Spirit According to St Thomas Aquinas*, Catholic Information Service, New Haven, CT, USA, 2002, p5, citing St Louis de Montfort's spiritual classic *True Devotion to Mary*, TAN Books, Gastonia, NC, USA, 2010.

205. Ibid. p32.

206. Steve Shawl, *The Medjugorje Messages*, Medjugorje Web, DeKalb IL, USA, 2019, p218.

207. Joseph Iannuzzi, *The Splendor of Creation*, St Andrew's Productions, McKees Rocks, PA, USA, 2004, p80.

208. Stefano Gobbi, *Our Lady's Beloved Sons*, Marion Movement of Priests, St Francis ME, USA, 1998, p1108.

209. Mirjana Soldo, *My Heart Will Triumph*, CatholicShop Publishing, Cocoa, FL, USA, 2016, p208.

210. Steve Shawl, *The Medjugorje Messages*, Medjugorje Web, DeKalb IL, USA, 2019, p44.

211. Wayne Weible, *Medjugorje: The Last Apparition – How It Will Change the World*, New Hope Press, Hiawassee, GA, USA, 2013, p226.

212. Ibid. p227.

213. Jason Hickel, *The Divide: A Brief Guide to Global Inequality and its Solutions,* William Heinemann Publishers, London, England, UK, 2017, p277.

214. David Spratt and Ian Dunlop, *Existential climate-related security risk,* Breakthrough – National Centre for Climate Restoration, Melbourne, Australia, 2019, pp6-9.

215. Jason Hickel, *The Divide: A Brief Guide to Global Inequality and its Solutions,* William Heinemann Publishers, London, England, UK, 2017, pp276-7.

216. Ibid. p280.

217. Joseph Cardinal Ratzinger, *Truth and Tolerance: Christian Belief and World Religions,* Ignatius Press, San Francisco, CA, USA, 2003, p142.

218. Ibid. p144.

219. Joseph Iannuzzi, *The Splendor of Creation,* St Andrew's Productions, McKees Rocks PA, USA, 2004, p181.

220. Marianne Trouve (ed), *The Sixteen Documents of Vatican II,* Pauline Books, Boston, MA, USA, 1999, p188.

221. HM Manteau-Bonamy, *Immaculate Conception and the Holy Spirit,* Franciscan Marytown Press, Libertyville, IL, USA, 2017, p174.

222. Mirjana Soldo, *My Heart Will Triumph,* CatholicShop Publishing, Cocoa, FL, USA, 2016, p145.

223. Mario Vasilj, *Medjugorje: Our Lady's Apostles – Vicka's Testimony,* Ogranak Matice Hrvatske, Citluk Medjugorje, Bosnia & Herzegovina, 2016, p2.

224. Nick Donnelly, *Who is the Devil: What Pope Francis Says?* CTC Publications, London UK, 2014, p27.

225. Richard Rohr, *On the Threshold of Transformation*, Loyola Press, IL, USA, 2010, p365.

226. David Smith, 'The US politics sketch', *The Guardian*, Washington, DC, USA, November 15, 2020.

227. Pope Francis with Austen Ivereigh, *Let Us Dream: The Path to a Better Future*, Simon & Schuster, London, UK, 2020, p135.

228. Commonwealth of Australia, 'State of the Climate 2020', CSIRO and the Bureau of Meteorology, Canberra, ACT, Australia, November 12, 2020.

229. Stephen Leahy, 'Greenland's ice is melting four times faster than we thought', *National Geographic Magazine*, Washington, DC, USA, January 2019.

230. Cindy Wooden (Catholic News Service), 'Pope Francis writes new prayers, asks Catholics to pray Rosary in May', *America Magazine*, New York, NY, USA, April 2020.

231. Mirjana Soldo, *My Heart Will Triumph*, CatholicShop Publishing, Cocoa, FL, USA, 2016, p369.

232. Congregation for the Doctrine of the Faith, 'Responsum to a dubium regarding the blessing of unions of persons of the same sex', *Holy See Press Office*, Vatican City, March 15, 2021.

233. Monica Dux, *Lapsed: Losing your religion is harder than it looks*, ABC Books/Harper Collins Publishers, Sydney, NSW, Australia, 2021, p174.

234. Ingrid Bretherton and Others, 'The Health and Well-Being of Transgender Australians: A National Community Survey', *LGBT Health*, cited in 'Why have nearly

half of transgender Australians attempted suicide', Melbourne University, Victoria, Australia, March 23, 2021.

235. Steve Shawl, *The Medjugorje Messages*, Medjugorje Web, DeKalb, IL, USA, 2019, p25.

236. Pope Francis, General Audience, San Damaso Courtyard, Apostolic Palace, Holy See, Vatican City State, June 23, 2021.

237. Media Release, 'Make time to unite with Pope Francis in prayer', Australian Catholic Bishops Conference, Canberra, ACT, Australia, March 18, 2022.

238. https://www.aljazeera.com/news/2022/3/17/scum-and-traitors-vladimir-putin-threatens-anti-war-russians

239. Mikhail Khodorkovsky, 'No end in sight', The Economist, Vol 442 No 9288, Mar 19, 2022.

240. Mirjana Soldo, My Heart Will Triumph, CatholicShop Publishing, Cocoa, FL, USA, 2016, p155.

241. https://www.republicworld.com/world-news/russia-ukraine-crisis/russian-orthodox-bishop-kirill-blames-ukraine-war-on-western-culture-and-gay-pride-parades-articleshow.html

242. https://religiondispatches.org/is-putin-a-real-christian-to-understand-this-conflict-we-need-to-ask-different-questions/

243. George Cardinal Pell, Email to the author from the Seminary of the Good Shepherd, Homebush, NSW, Australia, June 16, 2020.

244. Rod Bower, Eulogy given at the Vigil Mass for Bishop Bede Heather, St Michael's Catholic Church, Baulkham Hills, NSW, Australia, March 3, 2021.

Selected Bibliography

John Allen, *The Francis Miracle*, Time Books Inc, New York, NY, USA, 2015.

Andrew Apostoli, *Fatima for Today*, Ignatius Press, San Francisco, CA, USA, 2010.

David Attenborough, *Our Planet*, a film series for Netflix by Alastair Fothergill and Keith Scholey, London, England, UK, 2019.

David Attenborough with Johan Rockstrom, *Breaking Boundaries: the Science of Our Planet*, a film for Netflix by Alastair Fothergill and Keith Scholey, London, England, UK, 2021.

Natale Benazzi (ed), *Pope Francis: Happiness in This Life*, Bluebird Books, London, England, UK, 2018.

Tarcisio Cardinal Bertone, *The Last Secret of Fatima*, Image Books, New York, NY, USA, 2008.

Frank Brennan, *Acting on Conscience*, University of Queensland Press, St Lucia, Qld, Australia, 2007.

John Cornwell, *Powers of Darkness, Powers of Light*, Viking Books, London, England, UK, 1991.

Joan Carroll Cruz, *See How She Loves Us: 50 Approved Apparitions of Our Lady*, Tan Books, Charlotte, NC, USA, 2012.

Nick Donnelly, *Who is the Devil? What Pope Francis Says*, CTS Publications, London, England, UK, 2014.

Massimo Faggioli, *Joe Biden and Catholicism in the United States*, Bayard Publications, New London, CT, USA, 2021.

Pope Francis, *Laudato Si: On Care of Our Common Home*, Holy See, Vatican City State, 2015.

Pope Francis, *The Church of Mercy: A Vision for the Church*, Loyola Press, Chicago, IL, USA, 2014.

Pope Francis with Austen Ivereigh, *Let Us Dream: The Path to a Better Future*, Simon & Schuster, London, UK, 2020.

Pope Francis with Dominique Wolton, *Path to Change*, Bluebird Books, London, England, UK, 2017.

Zvonimir Gavranovic, *In Search of Cardinal Stepinac*, Krscanska Sadasnjost Press, Zagreb, Croatia, 2014.

Barry Hanratty, *Garabandal*, Garabandal Journal Publishing, St Cloud, MN, USA, 2018.

Joseph Iannuzzi, *The Splendor of Creation*, St Andrew's Productions, McKees Rocks, PA, USA, 2004.

Austen Ivereigh, 'Is Francis our first charismatic pope?' *America: the Jesuit Review*, New York, NY, USA, June 2019.

Francis Johnston, *Fatima: The Great Sign*, Augustine Publishing Company, Devon, England, UK, 1980.

Rene Laurentin, *Bernadette Speaks*, Pauline Books and Media, Boston, MA, USA, 2000.

Rene Laurentin & Michael Corteville, *Discovery of the Secret of La Salette*, Fayard Publications, Paris, France, 2002.

Vladimir Lenin, *Collected Works Vol 26*, 'The Russian Revolution and Civil War', Progress Publishers, Moscow, Russia, 1972.

CS Lewis, *Miracles*, Harper Collins Publishers, London, England, UK, 2012.

CS Lewis, *The Problem of Pain*, Harper Collins Publishers, London, England, UK, 2002.

CS Lewis, *The Screwtape Letters*, Time-Life Books Incorporated, Chicago, Il, USA, 1963.

Antonio Borelli Machado, *Fatima: The Unheeded Message*, The Australian TFP Bureau, Sydney, NSW, Australia, 2005.

Emmanuel Maillard, *The Hidden Child of Medjugorje*, Children of Medjugorje Inc, Medjugorje, Bosnia & Herzegovina, 2007.

HM Manteau-Bonamy, *Immaculate Conception and the Holy Spirit*, Marytown Press, Libertyville, IL, USA, 2008.

John de Marchi, *The True Story of Fatima*, The Fatima Center, Buffalo, NY, USA, 2009.

Frederic Martel, *In the Closet of the Vatican*, Bloomsbury Publishing, New York, NY, USA, 2019.

Emil Milat, Conversations with the Author, St Patrick's Church, Canberra, ACT, Australia, 2019.

TG Morrow, *Overcoming Sinful Anger*, Sophia Institute Press, Manchester, NH, USA, 2014.

Louis de Montfort, *True Devotion to Mary*, Tan Books and Publishers, Gastonia, NC, USA, 2010.

New Jerusalem Bible, *Reader's Edition*, Doubleday Publishing Group, New York, NY, USA, 1990.

George Cardinal Pell, Letters to the Author, Archdiocesan Chancery, Polding Centre, Sydney NSW, 2012.

Thomas W Petrisko, *The Fatima Prophecies*, St Andrews Productions, McKees Rocks, PA, USA, 1998.

Ailsa Piper, *Sinning Across Spain: Walking the Camino*, Victory Books, Melbourne, Australia, 2017.

Joseph Pronechen, 'Fatima's little-known miracles with earth and water', *National Catholic Register*, Kettering, OH, USA, Sep 2017.

Joseph Cardinal Ratzinger, 'The Message of Fatima', *L'Osservatore Romano: Weekly Edition in English*, Holy See, Vatican City State, June 2000.

Joseph Cardinal Ratzinger, *Truth and Tolerance: Christian Belief and World Religions*, Ignatius Press, San Francisco, CA, USA, 2004.

Richard Rohr, *On the Threshold of Transformation: Daily Meditations for Men*, Loyola Press, IL, USA, 2010.

Lucia dos Santos, *Fatima in Lucia's Own Words*, Pastoral Secretariat, Fatima, Portugal, 2000.

Russ Shafer-Landau, *Whatever Happened to Good and Evil?* Oxford University Press, New York, NY, USA, 2004.

Mirjana Soldo, *My Heart Will Triumph*, CatholicShop Publishing, Cocoa, FL, USA, 2016.

William Taubman, *Gorbachev: His Life and Times*, Simon & Schuster, London, England, UK, 2017.

Francois Trochu, *Saint Bernadette Soubirous*, Tan Books and Publishers, Rockford, IL, USA, 1985.

Marianne Trouve (ed), *The Sixteen Documents of Vatican II*, Pauline Books & Media, Boston, MA, USA, 1999.

Judith Weible, *Medjugorje Newsletter*, Weible Columns Publishing, Hiawassee, GA, USA, Apr 2020.

Wayne Weible, *Medjugorje: The Last Apparition – How it Will Change the World*, New Hope Press, Hiawassee, GA, USA, 2013.

George Weigel, *Witness to Hope: The Biography of Pope John Paul II*, Harper Collins Publishers, New York, NY, USA, 1999.

Paul Watson, *Defend Conserve Protect,* a film by Stephen Amis, Melbourne, Vic, Australia, 2019.

Philip Ziegler, *Militant Grace*, Baker Publishing Group, Grand Rapids, MI, USA, 2018.

Index

Made in the USA
Monee, IL
26 September 2022

14396835R00174